A Jew among the Evangelicals

A Guide for the Perplexed

Mark I. Pinsky

Westminster John Knox Press
LOUISVILLE • LONDON

Book design by Sharon Adams
Cover design by Eric Walljasper, Minneapolis, MN

First edition
Published by Westminster John Knox Press
Louisville, Kentucky

This book is printed on acid-free paper that meets the American National Standards Institute Z39.48 standard. ♾

PRINTED IN THE UNITED STATES OF AMERICA

06 07 08 09 10 11 12 13 14 15 — 10 9 8 7 6 5 4 3 2 1

Library of Congress Cataloging-in-Publication Data is on file at the Library of Congress, Washington, D.C.

ISBN-13: 978-0-664-23012-8
ISBN-10: 0-664-23012-1

For

Steven Engel, Jim Henry, Joel Hunter, Clark Whitten, Ernest
Bennett, and Bobby Welch
Men of Faith All, Who Helped Me Understand

and

In Memory of My Friend Bill Bright

Contents

Introduction

Suburban Odysseys

So," you might ask, "what's a nice Jewish boy from Jersey doing in the front pew of First Baptist Church of Orlando?" It's a fair question, and the answer is something of a tale. My circuitous trek has included the politically turbulent 1960s, when I was a campus radical, and sojourns in Israel, Ulster, Cuba, and China; marriage to a Gentile who agreed to raise our children as Jews; newspaper writing on both U.S. coasts; earthquakes and hurricanes; listening to stories of faith from people across the theological spectrum: some wild, some wacky, some wonderful.

I've sat in mosques, synagogues, temples, and churches, hearing sermon upon sermon—both boring and inspiring, boisterous and reserved. And I've come to know dedicated believers—of a faith different than mine—as personal friends and neighbors. The stories of this curious and unlikely journey, mostly among evangelical Christians, are humorous, entertaining, intriguing, touching, and illustrative of the vast landscape of American diversity.

This book tells these stories. If perhaps you are a journalist, as I am, you may see yourself in some of these tales. Regardless of your occupation, I hope you'll find laughter, perhaps puzzlement, and heartfelt interest in how people just like you wrestle with feelings, values, and beliefs that touch the core of their beings. And I hope you'll catch a glimpse of someone learning to understand and get along with folks whose convictions differ from his own. In fact, that reminds me of one esteemed religious leader I visited when he was near death. What happened was . . .

But I'm getting ahead of myself. I should start, as my forebear, Moses, wrote, "In the beginning . . ."

When I left my suburban, southern New Jersey home in 1965 to attend Duke University in Durham, North Carolina, I vowed I would never look back. I told my parents they could give my room to my younger brother, Paul, because I was finished with the suburbs. It wasn't that Pennsauken, New Jersey, was such a bad place. We didn't live in a treeless, cookie-cutter tract; our house was one of half a dozen new split-levels built in an older neighborhood. Although the area was all white, it wasn't completely homogeneous. In addition to the Jews, there were Protestants, Catholics, and Eastern Orthodox on our street, Irish, Italian, Polish, and Greek, most like us immigrants from the nearby city. What I rebelled against was the bland, boring, and predictable life I thought it was. There was no excitement. The cultural soil seemed as shallow as the sod unrolled on new yards, nurturing no music or history or literature of its own.

And so, for thirty years I was true to my pledge. I spent the better part of two decades on and around the Duke campus, where, in the late 1960s and early 1970s my political beliefs were shaped for the rest of my life. A column I wrote for the campus daily, the *Chronicle*, was called "The Readable Radical." I lived in dorm rooms, apartments, and houses in town and in the country. In the years I lived in North Carolina, I came to love the place. I understand what Eli N. Evans, a native of Durham, meant when he wrote in his classic memoir, *The Provincials: A Personal History of Jews in the South*: "I believe that no one born and raised in the South can escape its hold on the imagination. I was touched in childhood by its passions and myths, by its language and literature, by the heartbeat of its music, by the rhythm of its seasons and the beauty of its land, by the menacing fear of violence, by the complexities of race and religion, by the intensity of its history and the turbulence of its politics."

Graduate school at Columbia University took me to New York's East Village for nearly a year, and wanderlust—and a job as an editorial advisor to China's Xinhua News Agency—brought me to Beijing for fifteen months. In 1984, I went to work for the *Los Angeles Times*. My wife, Sallie, and I moved to Long Beach, two blocks from the Pacific in a small community called Belmont Shore, where our children, Asher and Liza, were born.

But in 1995 I left the *Times* to become religion writer for the

Orlando Sentinel in Central Florida. The southern California real estate market had been good to us, and so we had lots of choices when we went house hunting, this time with the kids in tow. Inevitably, I suppose, this led me back to the suburbs. We landed in a big house, among doctors and lawyers, clergy and college professors—most well above my journalist's pay grade. Sure, we were on the "poor" side of the street, away from the lake, but as I walked in the front door and looked up at the cathedral ceiling and imposing stone fireplace, I thought, "This is a house my parents should be living in, not me." The lesson: Be careful what you mock in your youth, lest you become it in middle age. I moved to the suburbs for the same reason I imagine my parents did; it seemed like a safe, happy environment in which to raise our children. Still, for an old campus firebrand, returning to the suburbs after all this time was disconcerting. A barbeque grill cost what a used car did in college. A new car went for what my parents paid for our house on Clayton Avenue. And a house—well, what can you say about a neighborhood where a short stroll across the street can bump the cost of a house by $750,000? With two Volvos in the driveway and relaxed-fit khakis as my daily wear, I suppose I had become the complete cliché—except that I consider myself a *Daily Show* Democrat, voting for the furthest left candidate on the ballot.

Soon, however, my old reporter's instincts kicked in, overriding the guilt. Or maybe it was those of a latent anthropologist. I realized that I had not simply returned to an upgraded, sunnier version of the suburbs of my Jersey youth. Looking at the broader context, I saw that many of my neighbors were evangelical Christians, and that their odyssey to the suburbs had been quite different from my own—not from the city, but from small towns and the rural countryside. In the years following World War II their parents and grandparents, often Southern Baptists or Pentecostals, had left the farm and the little church for the suburbs. This evolution was brought home to me one rainy Monday night in 2005 in Longwood, Florida, a suburb of Orlando, when I was taking a visiting writer, T. D. Allman, on a tour of the religious landscape. I was in the second row at Northland Church, a bustling congregation whose sanctuary is a converted roller-skating rink, for the last of seven regular weekend services. As the musical "praise team" pounded out a contemporary version of

"There Is Power in the Blood," with drums, guitars, and an electronic keyboard, it suddenly struck me that many of the forebears of those sitting around me probably sang a traditional version of the same hymn in some simple, clapboard church in the country. Now, across the Sunbelt, hundreds of thousands of others like those gathered at Northland also worship at slick modern megachurches with high-energy services, just as they shop at discount, warehouse stores. Meeting them outside my newspaper office, mingling with them in central Florida at PTA meetings and at Scouts, going to birthday and block parties in the decade I have spent here taught me a great deal about my Sunbelt neighbors, their faith, and their emerging political and cultural influence.

My own faith life, which began in a Conservative Jewish home, was also changing, and deepening. With our two children in grade school, my wife and I were becoming more involved in our own house of worship, the Congregation of Liberal Judaism in Orlando. For brief periods, when I took leave from work to start each of my first two books, I got up early each morning to pray at a nearby Ortho-dox synagogue, Congregation Ahavas Yisrael. Responding to some instinct, perhaps echoes of my late father's voice, I put on the leather phylacteries called teffilin for the first time in thirty-five years. There may have been other reasons for this return to Judaism that I did not recognize in the early years.

Jews in the Sunbelt, especially those outside large cities and aca-demic enclaves, tend to gather in synagogue congregations and community centers for religious and cultural self-defense, to pre-vent assimilation. While some do drift away from Judaism, others become more observant, or have spouses that convert. As a result of intermarriage and conversion, Jews here are almost as likely to be named Finley, Rodriguez, Rassmussen, or Aggarwal, as Schwartz or Cohen. Whatever the motivation, it must have been contagious. In 2005 my wife, Sallie, who was raised a Presbyterian, announced that she had decided to convert to Judaism. One of my Christian friends, Rusty Wright, a Campus Crusade for Christ alumnus, play-fully accuses me of practicing "Jewish evangelism." My response is that, if this is so, it is of a very laid-back variety. After twenty-four years of marriage—and not a mention of conversion from me in all that time—Sallie made her decision as an independent and a (very) critical thinker. I am pleased, and I know my parents would have been doubly pleased, but ours has always been a Jewish household, thanks to my wife.

For a journalist, the timing of our move to central Florida was doubly fortuitous. By the mid-1990s, the national media had dubbed Orlando "the new Peoria," an emblematic Sunbelt city, a service-based economy where the climate varied so little that the word "season" was more associated with sports and athletics than with weather. At the same time, for evangelicals, Orlando was becoming a "New Jerusalem"—a destination of choice for international ministries and parachurch organizations. Some, like Campus Crusade for Christ and Wycliffe Bible Translators, were cashing out of pricey California real estate. With their profits, they were buying large pieces of land for new headquarters and much better international air connections than the other "New Jerusalem," Colorado Springs, home of Focus on the Family and numerous other ministries.

Clearly I was in the right place at the right time. My evangelical education had begun.

Chapter 1

Sunbelt Evangelicals

Three Families

The evangelical Christians I have met over the past ten years in my life and my work, in Florida and throughout the Sunbelt, are quite different from the Methodists, Presbyterians, Lutherans, Baptists, Episcopalians, and Catholics I grew up with and went to school with in New Jersey. Like members of most mainline denominations, the northeasterners accepted religious pluralism as a given, respecting the settled beliefs—and, more critically, the nonbeliefs—of others. Of course they welcomed all to their congregations, but their preferred method of spreading Christianity was by example, by modeling their faith. Their theology was moderate—even liberal—intellectually rational, and emotionally restrained. "The liberal worldview emphasizes negotiated relationships, rather than timeless templates," Doug Muder wrote in *UU World*, the magazine of the Unitarian Universalist Association of Congregations. For them, the Bible was the inspired word of God, rather than literal Holy Writ. And for many mainline Christians this approach seems to be working quite well. "One of the best-kept secrets in American society," Muder wrote, "is that religious liberal families are holding together at least as well as any other kind of family."

The social gospel has always been central to the belief and practice of mainline Protestantism. For more than 125 years, beginning about 1840, the northern branches of their denominations were at the forefront of the nation's great social, economic, and political campaigns: abolition of slavery, women's voting rights, unions and child labor laws, Prohibition, civil rights, nuclear disarmament, peace, equal rights for women, and an end to discrimination based on sexual orientation. But these denominations have one other big thing in common: For the past two decades, with scattered exceptions, they appear to be running out of steam—aging, losing members, and deeply divided over the issue of homosexuality. This is not to say that there aren't vibrant, growing congregations in each of these denominations; there are many. But the membership trend lines are in seemingly inexorable decline, including Catholics, absent the infusion of immigrants.

If these are mainline Christians, who then are the Sunbelt evangelicals? They are people who define themselves primarily by their faith and religious commitment. They are called evangelicals because the core of their identity is linked to two verses in the New Testament, Matthew 28:19–20: "Go therefore and make disciples of all nations, baptizing them in the name of the Father and of the Son and of the Holy Spirit, teaching them to observe all that I have commanded you; and lo, I am with you always, to the close of the age" (RSV). While they adhere to a conservative theology, and most believe that the Bible is inerrant (literally without error), it is this "Great Commission" that unites them and defines them as evangelicals. Actively spreading their faith is essential. Often they belong to independent, unaffiliated churches, but some are members of conservative denominations like the Southern Baptist Convention, the Assemblies of God, and the Lutheran Church—Missouri Synod. And, in the Sunbelt, many also attend churches in mainline denominations, like Presbyterians and Episcopalians, that were once divided by their views on slavery.

Evangelicals tend to spend a good deal of time with their congregations—49 percent of the nation's megachurches are in the South, according to a 2006 survey conducted by Hartford Seminary—including Wednesday evenings and home Bible study groups other days during the week. They will often tithe—donate the Bible's "tenth portion" of their gross income to the church or to religious causes. Begun in revival in the early twentieth century, the American movement then known as fundamentalism eschewed political activity and engagement with the popular culture of the day. This changed in the early 1980s, largely as a reaction to changes in American society that took place in the 1960s, when fundamentalists transformed themselves into—or were eclipsed by—Christians who called themselves "evangelicals." Politically engaged, they prefer to rely on relationships and obligations based on family, church, and shared theological views, rather than those determined by secular and societal choice. Their values tend to be absolute and not relative, traditional rather than modern or even postmodern, understood as given by God rather than developed by human beings.

Still, evangelicals are not immune from the changes in American culture, at least in the Sunbelt suburbs. For example, they are often very accepting of gay people on a personal level, although they consider homosexuality a sin, and the younger generation seems to be wobbling on that point. (A petition effort to put a constitutional amendment banning gay marriage in Florida—a measure opposed by Governor Jeb Bush because it is already against state law—fell 150,000 signatures short of qualifying for the November 2006 ballot.) They may preach a biblically patriarchal model of marriage, wives submitting to their husbands; but if you look closely enough, they seem to be practicing the egalitarian model their self-proclaimed representatives are so quick to condemn. While they may exalt stay-at-home moms, economic need, including paying for Christian school tuition, may require the wife to work outside the home. This gap between what is preached and what is practiced is even more evident at the higher levels of evangelical Christianity. I can recall press conferences at the annual Southern Baptist Convention where leaders of the denominations explained their positions on wifely submission and why women senior pastors were a bad idea. Next to them sat their spouses—each one an author, broadcaster, and/or motivational speaker. As the Romans said, *res ipsa loquitur*, "the thing speaks for itself."

Thad and Virginia Knowles have ten children, ranging from infancy to eighteen, all their biological offspring and all home-schooled. The family lives in a blue stucco house in an older suburban development located in unincorporated Seminole County, which borders on Orange County. Thad, forty-six, oversees a modest family trust, but spent a number of years working in his father's civil engineering firm and as a facility manager for the large downtown YMCA. Virginia, forty-two, is in charge of the children's education; she is also the author and publisher of three home-school books.

Most of their well-mannered and articulate children ringed the living room when I came to interview them, a few coming and going, as a scented candle burned on a small table. Earlier on the Sunday I visited them, they had dedicated their three-month-old daughter, Melody, at Metro Life Church in Casselberry, where the family worships. Before the baby's birth, Virginia pledged to forgo an epidural pain-blocker during childbirth, in order to send part of the $1,600 out-of-pocket payment she would save to an African pastor in Malawi. But during labor, as sometimes happens to those choosing natural childbirth, she had a change of heart. Facing what she thought would be hours of excruciating pain, Virginia called for an anesthesiologist. But Melody arrived before the doctor, and the African minister received $500. Another $500 went to hurricane relief a few weeks later. These are *serious* Christians.

The parents' decision to educate their children at home, along with their Christian faith, dominates their life. Virginia emphasized that their choice was "a vision for what we *did* want to do rather than a reaction to negative elements we saw in the public schools. We wanted to build relationships as we learned along with our children, and customize their education to their interests and abilities, and to our Christian beliefs." For example, they believe in "young earth" creationism, that God created the earth about six thousand years ago. Still, they appear to be doing a successful job. Their home schooling is not orthodox or absolute; the two oldest daughters took courses at the local community college while still in high school. When the subject matter got beyond Virginia's level of competence, the older children took upper-level classes through various Christian home-school programs. Julia, sixteen, also plays forward on the church's girls' varsity basketball team. Mary, at eighteen the oldest, took advanced placement English through the state of Florida's online studies program and earned the highest grade possible in the standardized exam. She is now on full scholarship in the honors college at the University of Central Florida.

Like many Sunbelt evangelicals, Virginia and Thad's journey to their present level of religious commitment was not a straight line. Virginia grew up in a nonreligious San Francisco home in the free-spirited 1970s and regretfully remembers many "immoral influences" mixed along with the great cultural experiences. When an aunt from Pennsylvania wrote to tell her family that she had become a Christian, "we thought she was off her rocker," Virginia recalled. "I remember running into pushy Christians, and I did not like them at all." But a cross-country family trip brought Virginia's family to the aunt's home, where they found that the woman's daughter, Virginia's cousin, had also become a Christian. "I was struck by the peace and joy in her life," Virginia said, transforming the aunt from someone who had always been a very angry person. "I became very aware of my own sin and guilt, and I was struck by how much I needed a savior. I'm so thankful to continue growing spiritually through daily prayer and Bible study." The following year, when her parents moved the family to Baltimore, Virginia began attending an evangelical church with a school friend. She took mission trips to Scotland and Israel, and eventually followed a boyfriend to central Florida, where she worked her way through UCF.

Thad was raised in a nominally religious Catholic-Episcopalian home, but became interested in evangelical Christianity through a former girlfriend while he was studying at the University of Kansas in the late 1970s. "I did not live a very God-honoring life as a young teenager, but while I was in college I realized that I needed Christ, who had died for all of my sins," he said. After graduating from college, he joined his father's firm in central Florida. He met Virginia at Northland Church, where they were married by the new young pastor, Joel Hunter. They lived for a time near Washington, D.C., but then returned to central Florida and Northland.

In 2002, the family settled in at Metro Life, a contemporary yet conservative congregation of about eight hundred a short drive from their home. Thad and Virginia attend a weeknight home study and prayer group. They are actively involved in most of the church meetings their children attend, whether it is leading a Royal Rangers boys' club or joining in on a monthly high-energy youth gathering. The Knowles teens, like most of the young people at Metro Life, do not date, instead reserving romantic relationships for serious prospects when they are of marriageable age. However, they enjoy hanging out in groups. The two oldest girls have also gone on short mission trips to Bolivia.

Politically, the family supports candidates that reflect their social views, especially their strong opposition to abortion and stem-cell research. The parents said they generally approve of the death penalty, and they are not big fans of the United Nations, but they admitted to mixed feelings about the Iraq war and school vouchers. However, both Virginia and Thad part company with many evangelicals on end-of-life issues. They were torn by the Terri Schiavo issue, with sympathy for those on both sides of the debate. Realizing that most government intervention can be prevented in cases like this, they have signed living wills stating their wish not to remain in a persistent vegetative state, and to forgo feeding tubes or water. Although Virginia said they "are not hugely political people," they campaigned as a family for George Bush in 2004. They remind their children not to make hasty negative judgments about Democrats and their programs, noting that they are fortunate to live in a nation built by all kinds of people working together. The three oldest girls are more partisan supporters of the GOP, but for similar issue-related reasons. "The Republicans seem to make more sense," said Rachel, fourteen, who is responsible for putting the Bush-Cheney bumper sticker on the family's white van.

The family's relationship with technology and culture is complex. At times, they will disconnect the antenna to the television, but at other times they will watch shows like *The Amazing Race*, *NUMB3RS*, *Lost*, and the occasional game show. "We definitely control what we watch," Virginia said, noting that the younger children stick to educational and Christian programs. The family's three computers are in constant use for school, business, and entertainment. A former computer programmer, Virginia has an Internet Web log and an online newsletter, both dealing with home-school issues for Christians. They screen movies on Christian Web sites before deciding whether to see them at the theater or rent them; "We're just kind of cautious," Thad explained. *Lord of the Rings* was a favorite with a few of the children. Thad and Virginia tend to choose movies on social justice topics, such as *Hotel Rwanda*. The family usually listens to Contemporary Christian Music on CDs or the radio, but Mary occasionally will listen to secular music while driving, as long as the banter and song lyrics are not too raw.

The biggest recent issue for the Knowles was where Mary would attend college. She was torn between staying home at UCF or attending The King's College in New York City, a school founded by Campus Crusade for Christ to train students to influence secular culture. Despite scholarships, there just wasn't enough money to go north to the Christian school. In the early days of her first semester in Orlando, Mary wondered if she had made the right decision, if her scholarship to the state university meant she was "getting poisoned for free." But she is now writing for the campus newspaper and is convinced she made the right choice. "I don't want to escape secular society," she said. "I don't want to live in a bubble. I'm coming in contact with ideas I don't agree with. That's what life is all about."

While finances are always a challenge, trust in the Divine keeps them going. "God is a faithful God," said Thad. "He provides for our needs. He will provide. That gives me faith to trust him—with children. I have seen God provide through many circumstances. That doesn't mean things are going to be easy, or that I'm not going to doubt." Understandably, medical costs are always a concern. Priced out of commercial health care, they have limited coverage through a Christian organization that enables members to pool resources to cover each others' medical expenses. For Virginia, their decision to have a large family and educate them at home requires "that we live rather simply. We try to be content with what we've got. We don't have to have the newest or the latest. I'm not that into materialism. That gives us the freedom to give away money." Because of their modest income and large number of dependents, the Knowles pay minimal federal taxes. They realize they are fortunate in this regard, and try to make up for it by making charitable donations when they can. "As evangelical Christians," Virginia concludes, "we are so thankful for all the resources we have, but we don't just want to be takers. Our heart is to give our lives away, just like Jesus did."

The Droppers family lives up the street from me. I see their toy beagle Duchess barking bravely from behind an invisible, electronic fence when I walk our own dogs each night. Lori and Karl have four children: Neil, eighteen; Jack, fifteen; Nina, thirteen; and Mara, ten. Another thing I noticed while walking the dogs is that there were often a number of cars parked in front of their brick house. I figured that these were various Scripture and youth groups, and I learned I was right. On a Sunday afternoon we talked around their dining room table, where a Bible rested as if it belonged.

The Droppers moved to central Florida more than nine years ago from western Michigan, where Lori and Karl met at Hope College, a

Christian school. Their relocation, for Karl's new job running the area's nationally known fitness center, was wrenching for Lori, who was raised in Michigan and left much of her family behind. The move also required a cultural adjustment, to the South, where family history can be important. "We're not from around here," Karl said. "We have no family here—zero roots. We worked hard to build Christian community." Said Lori, "In a way, we had to prove ourselves." It was less of a change theologically. Their background is the Reformed Church of America, with roots in the old Dutch Reformed Church, and they found a home at Northland, the nondenominational megachurch.

Karl, forty-five, is a barrel-chested man with a pro football player's build, and bears a passing resemblance to the actor Brian Dennehy. Yet the New Jersey native is surprisingly soft-spoken. Lori, forty-four, who says she took a "twelve-year sabbatical" to raise her children, has returned to work part-time as a physical therapist. Her smile is almost reflexive. The kids all attend public school, and most are members of the Fellowship of Christian Athletes—Neil is quarterback of the Winter Park High School football team. "We wanted to try public school until it was a problem, and it never was a problem," Lori said. "We feel called to be there, but we would change tomorrow if it was the right thing to do."

Faith and religion play a central role in the lives of family members. "It's something you can rely on to get through things," said Jack, who plays and composes Christian music. "You're a lot more comfortable with friends who are Christians." At the same time, he volunteered, one of his closest friends is not a Christian, and he tries not to overwhelm him with Christianity. For Neil, "Christianity dictates how I live my life. It's there to turn to, as a comfort. It dictates how I deal with other people." Nina and Mara find it helps them make the right choices. Family members have made numerous mission trips to the Third World, singly and together: Jamaica, the Dominican Republic, and Egypt. Closer to home, their evangelism reflects their (mostly) midwestern background. "We try to live loud without saying anything," Lori said, explaining that they prefer to model their faith rather than to proclaim it to strangers. "It's the day-to-day walk," Karl added.

Politically, the Droppers are conservative, but not predictably so. Lori said that if she knows that the heart of a politician is Christian, "I trust him." Karl said, "I don't believe there's a party affiliation with Christianity, but I do believe there is a correlation with the decision-making process." They are staunchly antiabortion but would consider an exception to save the life of the mother. And they are opposed to gay marriage, although Karl said he wouldn't fight or vote against some form of civil union. Both parents think school vouchers would be all right, but they are not at the top of their list of priorities. The way evolution is taught in schools "is not worth my argument," Karl said. "What matters to me is that God created the earth," Lori said, not when creation took place. Their faith leads them to oppose the death penalty, but not in any sustained way, and they admit they might feel differently if a member of their own family was a victim. They feel the burden of helping those less fortunate, or in distress, should be more on the church than on the government. Lori said, when it comes to the environment, that "we are stewards of this world," yet the rights of human beings are greater that any threatened species of slug.

The Droppers engage popular culture cautiously. They have rules: no PG-13 movies until the age of thirteen, and not always then; no R-rated movies until seventeen. Still, the parents encourage the children to make decisions in this area on their own, where possible. "We want you to think about it and decide," Lori said to her children around the table, and this approach seems to have worked with her children. "You can hide yourself in the world by only listening to Christian music or reading Christian books," Jack said. "Listening to secular music is fine as long as you don't let it take over your life." Neil, his older brother, agreed, saying he "listens to music and watches movies for entertainment value." Nina said, despite the provocative fashions on television and in magazines, "I try not to let it influence me in what I do or how I dress." When Mara, the youngest, wanted to read the first Harry Potter book, Lori read it first and then read it again with her daughter.

I asked Karl if he thought his faith influenced the way he did his high-profile job. "It manifests itself in what kind of person Karl Droppers is," he said. Churches and faith-based organizations use his facility, and the operators of the complex host and sponsor evangelical events. Yet Christian employees sometimes ask why he isn't more "out there" about his faith, since "we have these resources to be used for the kingdom." But Karl has had to step in when subordinates bring an agenda, even a religious one, to the workplace. "We can't allow people to use this as a platform," he said. "We cannot allow that. It has happened." He said he has prayed for people he has had to fire, and he acknowledged that he saw no difference in the work perform-ance of Christian and non-Christian employees.

In the marriage dynamic, Lori said that recognizing her husband as the head of the household "works better," even if it seems old-fashioned. "He doesn't make me feel unequal. It's just a different role." Ironically, Karl said he "leans toward the egalitarian way. You like to come to a joint decision. You don't always get there."

In many ways, JoJo and Michael Dey are also typical evangelicals. Next to the entrance of their home, on the doorpost where Jews tra-ditionally put a mezuzah, is a stylized cross. I met them through JoJo and their teenaged daughter Sarah, who are members of my wife's book club for mothers and daughters. Michael was raised a Southern Baptist, but he and his wife are now active members of All Saints Episcopal Church in Winter Park, where both are former Sunday school teachers and JoJo served on the governing vestry. Although Episcopal Church members elsewhere in the nation may not be con-sidered evangelicals, in the South many are. The Deys are firmly in their denomination's conservative camp, opposing the blessing of same-sex unions and the ordination of sexually active gay priests. The couple devotes about ten hours a week to their church and religious activities, and they tithe. By any definition, they are devout Chris-tians. Both pray daily, beginning early in the morning, and belong to weekday Bible study groups. Michael also participates in an online Bible study and, on the way to work, he listens to an old-time radio preacher on the Christian radio station.

The Deys also bring their faith with them to their jobs, where each sees the more problematic side of life at close range. So it is not sur-prising that they support the need for increased government involve-ment in solving those problems. This distinguishes them from the more typical evangelical family in the adjoining pew, whose experi-ence and livelihood are more in the private sector. "I pray during the day, as I need to," Michael said. "I reflect on whether I see God's hand in things." While he mixes easily with "good ole boys," he is a pro-gram administrator for the health department, running the Orange

County AIDS program, and he has been immersed in social service work for most of his life. If clients ask him about his faith, he shares it. "I talk about how important my faith is for me. I tell them I have a sense that God is looking out for me." JoJo is a licensed marriage and family therapist working part-time doing family counseling, under her maiden name. If, in the course of her work, faith or theology arises, JoJo will explain to her counseling clients that her Christianity guides her. "I view the world through the lens of my faith," she tells them. "That is going to shape my advice to you." At the same time, she said she does not evangelize in a formal sense. "For example, if working with a couple I may describe what a 'covenant marriage' looks like and how it is different from a 'contractual marriage.'"

Unlike many in the evangelical community Michael and JoJo married relatively late: he was thirty-seven; she was twenty-nine. Both had spent many years during the 1970s and '80s as socially active singles, although Michael had been married before. They are staunchly pro-life, opposing abortion except when the life of the mother is clearly at stake. They adopted their daughter, Sarah, now fourteen, when she was five days old, through a Christian adoption agency. In addition to raising Sarah, they have waged a grueling and expensive campaign to adopt the elementary school–age grandson of JoJo's stepmother, named Daniel. The boy's parents were in and out of the legal system, mostly with drug problems, until his father died. It was a decision that did not come easily for the couple, now that they are in their forties and fifties. "We prayed about it for months," Michael said, sitting with his wife in the family living room one Sunday afternoon. "My faith walk enabled me to make my decision to invite Daniel into our family," said JoJo. Her faith is the mechanism by which she makes her decisions. Sometimes, while driving Sarah and Daniel to school, they will pray about pressing issues the kids may be facing that day. Still, neither Michael nor JoJo actively proselytize. Their daughter, who attends public school, is the family's designated "prayer warrior," the parents agreed. She is an active member of the Fellowship of Christian Athletes and a member of All Saints' youth outreach group. JoJo said that Sarah probably dresses more conservatively than most of her peers—favoring Christian-themed T-shirts. The parents take a fairly hard line on popular culture, monitoring their children's movies and television viewing. They are fans of the animated series of videos and DVDs called VeggieTales, Contemporary Christian Music, and the local Christian rock station. But mother and daughter also enjoy watching WB's *Gilmore Girls* together. Michael and JoJo made it halfway through the Left Behind series of novels before losing interest in the Apocalypse.

Some things about the Deys are not predictable. They oppose the Iraq war, which JoJo calls "an abomination. It's Bush's shame. Bush has sold it as a Holy War. It breaks my heart. And yet we are demonized if we voice our opposition. It's as if we're un-American if we're against this war." Their position on the death penalty is much like the Droppers; they are against it, but they too admit that if the victim were a family member, they might feel differently. While they oppose gay marriage, they have no objection to some form of civil union. They support trade unions and think government needs to do and fund more programs, and if that means higher taxes, so be it. "Our obligation is to aid the poor, both as individuals and through the government," Michael said. "I'm happy to pay more, if we need to, to make our country a better place." JoJo agrees. "We *are* the government. People vote people into office. We are responsible for choosing who are making our decisions. Individuals and the government have an equal responsibility. The government has the big picture—they see the gaps—and can be the vehicle to fill those gaps." They are against school vouchers. "I hate to see anything that takes away from public education," Michael said. "I don't think the voucher system is the way to go." His position on the earth's origins is probably reflective of many educated, suburban evangelicals. "The science of evolution is pretty solid. I believe the science. But I also believe in Genesis—I just don't know how they fit together." Their view of marriage is likewise syncretic: They see it as an egalitarian partnership, but JoJo said if there was a serious disagreement, she would probably yield to Michael, once he "knew her heart."

Politically, the Deys are *very* different evangelicals. As their positions on various issues suggest, both Deys think "Bush" is a four-letter word. They are proud and feisty Democrats living among a sea of Republicans in their Maitland neighborhood—one of the area's most outspoken and conservative evangelists lives around the corner—and in their church. In the driveway, their minivan sports a bumper sticker reading, "I'm a Christian and a Democrat." However, they also understand how out of step they are with those with whom they associate. JoJo once estimated that of the hundreds in her weekly Bible study group, about 2 percent are Democrats. Said Michael: "Democrats tend to be quiet because they feel judged."

I try not to lose sight of any of these families, and others like them, when I go to work each morning at the *Orlando Sentinel* to explain them to the world, and to each other.

Chapter 2

Among the Evangelicals

*T*he suburbs are the heart and political center of gravity of Sunbelt Christianity, a movement that increasingly sets the tone for American life. Current media stereotype notwithstanding, there is more to the region's suburban living than overweight people driving overweight vehicles, making safe, personal choices while largely unconcerned about the larger world. There is also a lot more to Sunbelt Christianity than a clamoring crusade by evangelicals with torches and pitchforks to impose a theocracy on the United States. "Evangelicals are as diverse as the general population of America," Rev. Ted Haggard, president of the National Association of Evangelicals, told Tom Brokaw, on NBC-TV's "In God They Trust," broadcast on October 28, 2005. "There's no one that's leading the megachurch movement or involved in the megachurch movement, that is in favor of theocracy. None of us are for that. We're all defenders of freedom and liberty for all."

Sunbelt Christianity is a new movement, distinct in many ways from its fundamentalist precursor, Bible Belt Christianity, which was largely rural, small-town, solidly Democratic, often racist, and anchored in the Deep South. I should also acknowledge that there are millions of African American, Hispanic, and working-class white evangelicals. However, my focus is on middle-class white evangelicals living in the Sunbelt suburbs—and, increasingly, the second-ring exurbs—because this critical demographic determines the outcome of elections. And also because these are the people I live among and know best. On many cultural and economic issues, such as tax policy, suburban Sunbelt evangelicals probably have more in common

15

with suburbanites in blue states that voted for John Kerry in 2004 than they do with rural and working-class evangelicals. Regardless of the theological source of their value systems, most suburban blue-staters live ethical, moral, and fruitful lives. Like their red-state counterparts who voted Republican in 2004, they believe that faithful marriage and a nuclear family are the ideal; that abortion should be avoided, if possible; that the growing coarseness of popular culture is deplorable; and that education is the surest road to advancement. "Religious conservatives and liberals share more concerns and beliefs than either commonly admits," wrote Doug Muder, in the Fall 2005 issue of *UU World*. "Both have loyalties beyond self and the convenience of the moment. . . . Both seek something more substantial than the momentary satisfaction of desire or the endless striving after status. The committed life is a different way to pursue these goals, not a denial of them."

Undeniably, there are strains of weirdness and wackiness in the way evangelical religion and culture are intertwined in the red states. How else can you explain a cell phone tower on the grounds of Ridge Assembly of God in Davenport, Florida, in the shape of a cross 175 feet tall and 80 feet across? Or Creation Expeditions, a Christian research organization and ministry based in Crystal River, Florida, where fossilized dinosaur bones and archeological digs are used to "prove" the biblical thesis that the world is only six thousand years old. Or a March 2005 press release from Shingle Creek Golf Club in Orlando announcing an Easter sunrise service overlooking the greens, followed immediately by the first annual "Easter Egg Scramble" golf tournament, bracketed by a buffet breakfast and Easter lunch? Sponsors described the Scramble as "a tournament and day complete with the solemnity that marks the occasion along with the joy associated with a round of golf." The service was free; the remainder of the package was $57.95 per person.

Not far removed from this wackiness is America's fictional evangelical next door. Pressed to identify a single member of this tribe who is not a national religious leader, a country music star, a politician, or an athlete, many people outside the Sunbelt would probably flail around like a desperate quiz show contestant—until the name Ned Flanders popped into their minds. Oddly enough, that animated character in *The Simpsons* wouldn't be such a bad choice. Like many of the voting Americans who determine the outcome of elections, the Flanders family says grace at meals, attends church most Sundays, reads and refers to the Bible, and prays out loud. Amid the lingering bewilderment in the wake of the 2004 presidential election, I can sympathize with those still puzzling over the evangelical enigma, especially my colleagues in the media. It's never easy to "parachute" into an alien environment and file a coherent story eight hours later. Like Boston journalists covering the Catholic Church or those in Salt Lake City covering the Mormons, those reporting about evangelicals while living in the Sunbelt enjoy the luxury of home-field advantage and the ability to return to the story again and again. When I began covering religion for the *Los Angeles Times* in Orange County in 1985, I knew very little about Sunbelt Christianity. As a Jew born in Miami and raised in the northeast suburbs, I first read the New Testament in a college course, and only because it was then required at my historically Methodist university. But over a decade at the *Times* covering this growing (and, to me, strange) tribe of people called evangelicals I learned a lot—or so I thought. Since this was the era of the televangelism scandals and I had done a good deal of investigative reporting, I focused on religious broadcasting, the outlets based in southern California—like Robert Schuller's *Hour of Power* and Paul Crouch's Trinity Broadcasting Network, that knit together the nation's evangelical community. Through them, I reasoned, I could better understand their viewers.

At the time, this top-down approach to the beat seemed logical. I was working in Orange County, but I lived in a quaint, cosmopolitan beach community in Los Angeles County, and so I had little visceral sense of what was happening at the evangelical grass roots in my circulation area. In retrospect, it is clear that I should have been paying closer attention to another, equally important story in my backyard: a little congregation in southern Orange County called Saddleback Church, which would grow into one of the nation's most influential megachurches. Its pastor, Reverend Rick Warren, whom I confess I never sought out to interview, developed the motivational concept of the forty-day Purpose-Driven Church. His subsequent and even more popular Purpose-Driven Life theme has in recent years swept the nation's congregations and, in book form, became a fixture on the bestseller lists.

Moving to the other end of the Sunbelt in 1995 to cover religion for the *Orlando Sentinel,* I didn't have the opportunity to make the same mistake. While evangelicals are *part* of a varied theological landscape in California, they *are* the landscape in Florida: Southern Baptists, Pentecostals, charismatic Catholics, and even many mainline Protestants—Presbyterians, United Methodists, Episcopalians, and Lutherans chief among them. Suddenly, I found myself in a very different Orange County. The most ubiquitous bumper sticker was not for a commercial rock station; it was for a station devoted to contemporary Christian music, and it was not uncommon to see them in the parking lot of the local Whole Foods market (or of my own newspaper). For the first time in my life, I was living in a sea of actively believing Christians, and the cold shock felt like total immersion. Still, reflexively, I returned to my top-down reporting ways, making up for lost time by doing articles about influential parachurch organizations based in Orlando. As on the West Coast, I learned a lot on the job, interviewing ministers, leaders, and laypeople. I attended church services more often than many Christians—some months more often than I attended my own synagogue. But the most intense part of my education came outside the job, without the mediation of a reporter's notebook. In the supermarket checkout line and in my neighborhood I encountered evangelicals simply as people, rather than as subjects or sources of quotes for my stories. We sat next to each other in the bleachers while the kids played recreational sports. Our family doctor went on frequent mission trips and kept a New Testament in the examining room. In the process, I learned even more about the Great Commission, the biblical obligation of all Christians to share their faith with the once-born and the unsaved.

Evangelicals were no longer caricatures or abstractions. I was able to interpret their metaphors and read their body language. From this personal, day-to-day experience I observed that evangelicals are not monolithic. Nor are they, as the *Washington Post* infamously characterized them in 1993, "poor, uneducated and easy to command." Like Ned Flanders, they are more likely to be overzealous than hypocritical, although there is certainly some of the latter. They don't march in lockstep to what Pat Robertson or Jerry Falwell or Focus on the Family's James Dobson tell them, and they hold surprisingly diverse views on many issues. While making common cause politically, their theological differences range from the subtle to the significant. This diversity is manifest in many ways. Southern Baptists oppose women in the pulpit, but Pentecostals do not. Conservative Catholics reject the use of condoms for birth control or in AIDS prevention, but many Protestants do not. Christian backing for Israel and its policies often comes with a galling and divisive price tag for American Jewish allies: simultaneous support by evangelicals for apostate Messianics who want to convert their faithful co-religionists and antithetical positions on domestic issues like abortion and separation of church and state. On the issue of Israel's territorial compromise, for example, many evangelicals are more militant than the hard-line Likud Party. "For so many of us," said Rabbi Aaron Rubinger, of Congregation Ohev Shalom in Orlando, "the major struggle has been weighing the great value of their strong support for Israel against their proselytizing efforts." While there is near unanimity opposing gay marriage and late-term abortion among evangelicals, serious and fundamental divisions exist over other issues, including the Iraq war and foreign policy, evolution, environmentalism, stem-cell research, capital punishment, tax policy, immigration, Social Security, government intervention in end-of-life issues—and yes, even civil unions. I know this in part because it is what the evangelicals I know tell me. There is also electoral diversity. Before the 2004 election, an evangelical woman in my wife's book club, a Democrat, jokingly referred to George Bush as "the antichrist."

There is ample statistical evidence to support this sense of diversity among the nation's estimated 50 million adult evangelicals. No one has paid more attention to this issue than John C. Green, director of the Ray Bliss Institute of Applied Politics at the University of Akron, who has conducted extensive research, especially on the attitudes of white evangelicals and conservative Catholics, the demographic pivot on which recent national elections have turned. (African Americans and Hispanics who identify themselves as evangelicals tend to vote Democratic, although by eroding margins.) I have attended Green's presentations around the country, consulted him numerous times by telephone for my articles, and frequently see and hear him on television and radio. "White evangelicals and conservative white Catholics have become the effective battleground for winning national elections," Green told me. "The single thing that Americans outside the Sunbelt and the Midwestern heartland fail to grasp about this key demographic is the diversity of their views. . . . The internal divisions within the evangelical tradition have largely escaped scholars and pundits alike."

In the spring of 2004, Green, who is also a senior fellow at the Pew Forum on Religion and Public Life, conducted the Fourth National Survey of Religion and Politics, "The American Religious Landscape and Political Attitudes." Financed by the Pew Forum, Green and his associates polled four thousand respondents in this quadrennial study, with a 2 percent margin of error. Follow-up surveys were taken after the 2004 presidential election. Despite all the postelection talk of the importance of values and social issues among those he calls religious "traditionalists," Green found that when they cast their votes, economics and foreign policy ranked higher in importance to them.

White evangelical voters—not confined to the Sunbelt—divided in their party allegiance in fairly predictable split: 56 percent Republican; 27 percent Democratic; 17 percent independent. The trend over time of Green's surveys is toward the GOP, with a similar rise in the importance of religion to political thinking, up to 58 percent. Ideologically, 55 percent identified themselves as conservative; 45 percent moderate or liberal. But on specific issues, Green found what many might consider some counterintuitive results, at least to blue-state residents. For example, only 49 percent said they felt close to the Christian Right. Among white evangelicals,·51 percent opposed free trade; 52 percent supported environmental regulations; 55 percent agreed that the wealthy should be taxed to fight poverty; 65 percent said that the United States should cooperate with international organizations, as opposed to taking the lead in foreign affairs; only 24 percent said that abortion should always be illegal, in all circumstances; 26 percent opposed the death penalty; 13 percent supported some form of civil union, and 12 percent said they support gay marriage; 45 percent said gays should have the same rights as other Americans; 43 percent opposed any ban on embryonic stem-cell research.

Green's findings were supported by other polls sponsored by the Pew Center for the People and the Press study conducted in December of 2004 and the Pew Forum on Religion and Public Life in July of 2005. The 2004 survey found that 69 percent of evangelical Protestants said it was more important to conduct embryonic stem-cell research than to protect embryos. That was up from 51 percent in a similar poll taken in

March of 2002. Even among those who said they attended weekly religious services, support for stem-cell research had risen from 28 percent to 38 percent during this same period. The 2005 Pew poll, which surveyed two thousand Americans, revealed that 21 percent of white Protestant evangelicals felt that Christian conservatives have gone too far in trying to impose their religious values on the country.

"Those considered the rigid Christian right are far more fluid than we think," a young Los Angeles evangelist named Erwin McManus told me.

Yes, abortion has been the paramount issue for evangelicals, but they are concerned about so much more. Many of their points are more left than right. The environment, diversity, social justice, poverty, peace and cooperation—all of these would resonate with the same people who are passionate pro-life. Why hasn't the media noticed that the world has changed, and so has the evangelical movement? The church across America is not what is portrayed in the media. The evangelical movement is not monolithic or monotonous! There are many new and diverse voices out there. I am an immigrant from El Salvador, raised in Miami, who represents a community of faith called Mosaic, in which sixty nationalities are represented, with an average age of twenty-six. Our congregation is filled with entrepreneurs, artists, innovators, and highly creative people. We think Mosaic is the future of the Christian movement, a future that is diverse, creative, compassionate, and global. Where is our voice? Everywhere but in the media!

There are some caveats to the Pew studies, and to McManus's views, according to my former *Orlando Sentinel* colleague and friend Peter A. Brown, former chief political correspondent for Scripps Howard and a man who knows about as much as anyone about reading and interpreting polls. "As large a cohort as they are, evangelicals are not a significant enough chunk of voters in Dixie to control elections," said Brown, himself a Jew and a New Yorker by birth who moved to central Florida a decade ago.

The GOP has become so dominant here because most of those who don't instinctively consider themselves Democrats—and even some who do—agree with the evangelicals on the issues that matter. I can't quibble with John Green's data, yet focusing on the specific issues obscures the big picture. People vote based on a small number of issues and instincts. For most, it is the big stuff—money and national security. And on those big issues, in the South, both evangelicals and other noncore Democrats think the same way.

And, while the influence of evangelicals may be most pronounced in the Sunbelt, where an increasing number of Americans are moving, Peter, who now surveys Florida for the Quinnipiac University Polling Institute, reminds me that there are also influential groups of evangelicals in the Rocky Mountain and Plains states, as well as in the lower Midwest.

Nevertheless, Green's findings reinforced my own personal experience with evangelicals. This epiphany—it would be hard to call it anything else, except maybe a revelation—changed the way I understood them. The fact that I do not agree with most evangelicals on political, cultural, or theological issues does not keep me from understanding, respecting, and accepting the sincerity of their beliefs. Living in central Florida made a difference in my reporting, enabling me to avoid the mistake I made by ignoring the rise of Rick Warren in California—and enabling me to finally meet and interview the evangelist in Orlando in 2005. I have been early in writing major articles on Houston's Joel Osteen and Brad Stine, the evangelical standup comedian. To a degree that might strike my blue-state friends as inexplicable, it has probably made me more sympathetic to them. I would like to say that this hard-earned understanding of evangelicals enables me to predict the outcome of the future elections, but I cannot. It didn't even enable me to predict the outcome of the 2004 presidential election. At the same time, President Bush's re-election did not leave me shell-shocked. We'll discuss this in more depth in Chapter 6.

I have had a good deal of contact with evangelicals and, though some leaders can be tendentious poseurs, I am grateful for most of what I find at eye level. For example, as an upper-middle-class parent of two teens, I am well aware of the dangers the suburbs can hold for young people: alcohol, drugs, sex, alienation, and antisocial behavior head a long list. No religious or ethnic group—including the Amish and Hasidic Jews—is immune from these temptations, whether living in the suburbs, cities, or rural areas. In July of 2005, for example, the mother of a teenaged boy told the Lake County, Florida, sheriff's department that her son had been sexually assaulted by three male high school students at a Fellowship of Christian Athletes football camp at a Southern Baptist conference center in the city of Leesburg. Nevertheless, some peer groups do seem less likely to succumb to the suburbs' temptations. That is why I was most at ease whenever my son and daughter spent time after school with evangelical Christians. As long as I was convinced there would be no proselytizing—no small concern for me—I was happy when they exchanged visits and attended each other's parties.

In 2004–2005, my son Asher and one of his friends from our temple joined a rock band with Charlie Kidd, a neighbor and friend of my son's from Trinity Preparatory School, where both were students. Charlie is the son of Reggie Kidd, a professor of New Testament at Reformed Theological Seminary in nearby Oviedo, Florida. I could just as easily have met Reggie doing a story for the *Orlando Sentinel,* but I didn't. As it happens, I first met him and his wife Shari in the gym stands at Maitland Middle School, where our kids were playing rec-league basketball. The Kidds hosted the band's earsplitting practice sessions with equanimity and unfeigned enthusiasm. Sometimes, I would slip into their study and chat while the band's rehearsals wound down. The Kidds seemed perfectly normal to me. By the same token, if I had to rent my house, furnished, for a year and hoped to get it back pretty much the way I'd left it, evangelical tenants would be high on my list of preferred tenants. But the thing I think I like most about this flavor of Christians is, if you are sorry, they have to forgive you.

Chapter 3

The Beat

"Do They Know You're Jewish?"

*D*o they know you're Jewish?"

My late father-in-law, Joe Brown, a longtime Presbyterian elder who died in 2005, would ask this question frequently over the years about my employers at the *Orlando Sentinel,* as well as about the people I cover as religion writer. He asked this question partly, I think, because he was amazed that I was doing *this* job in *this* part of the country—and partly because, in his eighties, he was getting a little forgetful. In any case, the answer was always yes. I know this because religion is probably the only beat in journalism where the people you interview feel free to ask about your faith and your religious affiliation before they allow the discussion to begin. The first time I interviewed Rev. Bobby Welch, pastor of First Baptist Church of Daytona Beach and then president of the Southern Baptist Convention, I was deep into an exposition about common problems I had observed facing Christian pastors. Welch was agreeing, and then interrupted the conversation to ask, "Are you an evangelical?" Well, not exactly, I replied.

This issue of disclosing your affiliation is a source of ongoing and sometimes heated debate whenever religion writers get together. Many of my colleagues are adamant about refusing to answer, arguing that it is no one's business and that, if answered directly, it is likely to skew the interview. I've made a different decision. Central Florida is an intensively, if not exclusively, evangelical area, which means many of the people I come in contact with are obligated by their religion's Great Commission to invite non-Christians to join

25

them in following Jesus. Thus, from a practical standpoint, it is important for them to know whether and how they should make that offer. On my side of the notepad, I need at least their undivided attention—if not their total candor. I don't want them to be distracted from my questions, trying to figure out what I am and when to make their pitch, when I am trying to get a straight answer. So at the outset of the first meeting I work into the conversation that I am a committed Jew—end of story. But their calculations have another, equally personal dimension. Many of the ministers of megachurches and heads of national and international religious organizations based in the Orlando area are quite media-savvy. Often as I have begun an interview, I could see they were trying to figure out the angle of the story, based on my political perspective. To clear the air, I would usually add that I am a left-wing Democrat and the brother of a Maryland state senator, in case they were wondering. A few were nonplused at what they considered a shocking admission, if not a confession, but most appeared relieved to know the framework of what was to come. After more than twenty years on the beat, my faith and my politics are now common knowledge in much of the evangelical world, as I hope is my reputation for fairness.

Another convention all journalists try to observe is to stay out of the story they are reporting. Sometimes that is unavoidable. The most persuasive person I have ever met on the religion beat was Bill Bright, founder of Campus Crusade for Christ. Physically unassuming—a small, round man and a bit of a dandy—he had a persistently beguiling way about him. He did not believe in targeting Jews for evangelism, he said, and he was emphatic that members of his organization should not be overbearing in their evangelism, that they should be gracious about accepting no for an answer. In the late 1990s, in an unguarded moment, I mentioned to him that there was some unease in central Florida's Jewish community, provoked by some recent incidents, one involving him, about their relations with the evangelical community.

In June of 1996, the Southern Baptist Convention, meeting in New Orleans, had voted money to support evangelism among the Jews. Specifically, the fourteen thousand delegates of the sixteen-million-member denomination resolved to "direct our energies and resources toward the proclamation of the Gospel to the Jews." At the urging of the Southern Baptist Messianic Fellowship, the denomination's Atlanta-based Home Mission Board gave Jim Sibley, of Criswell College in Dallas, the assignment of converting the Jews to Christianity. (That effort was renewed in 2005, when the denomination's executive committee recommended that the Southern Baptist Convention establish a formal mission to the Jews.) "My reaction is this is a great setback," Rabbi James Rudin, interreligious affairs director of the American Jewish Committee, told the *New York Times* on June 13, 1996. "By singling out Jews as a target for conversions, it's a great disservice not just to Baptist-Jewish relations but to Christian-Jewish relations." Rabbi Yechiel Eckstein, of Chicago, a longtime advocate of Jewish-evangelical amity, called the resolution "unnecessary, insensitive, offensive and inciteful. . . . It made Jews in America and abroad feel they were coming under siege and would be facing a major proselytizing assault from Christians." Billy Graham, the nation's best-known Southern Baptist, disavowed the action, as did leaders of other mainline Christian denominations. But the damage was done, especially in the Sunbelt, where Jews have often felt embattled and isolated. For the Jews of central Florida, threats like this were not theoretical. A ministry called Zion's Hope, also dedicated to converting the Jews, had located in Orlando and was building a new national headquarters there.

Later in 1996, in November, Jewish members of the Florida legislature objected when a minister invited by the Republican Speaker of the House of Representatives, who was from Orlando, invoked the name of Jesus Christ in his invocation at a special session, in apparent violation of the tradition of nonsectarian prayer. Then, in March of 1997, another Orlando legislator, Daniel Webster, invited Bright to deliver an invocation at the beginning of the Senate session. Bright prayed in the name of "the Lord Jesus Christ . . . the true God, the only God," which again upset Jewish legislators from predominately Democratic south Florida. Despite the fact that the session's benediction was delivered by Rabbi Merle Singer, of Boca Raton, others were also offended. "It seems to me they are shoving it in our faces," said Rabbi Stanley Garfein, of Tallahassee. Despite the protests, Webster, a favorite of the religious right then serving as Speaker of the House, said he would not "censor prayer." (In 2004, Webster, who had moved to the Senate, invited another Orlando pastor to deliver the invocation, with similar wording. Senate President Jim King, a fellow Republican, apologized to the chamber's six Jewish senators.)

Bright seemed genuinely dismayed by the incident and asked what he could do to repair the situation. Without thinking, I suggested he meet with my young rabbi, Steve Engel, then serving as president of the Greater Orlando Board of Rabbis. OK, Bright said, *you* set up a lunch meeting. I demurred, saying the contact should be direct, without me as an intermediary. Bright agreed, but a series of missed phone calls ensued, so Bright again asked me to intercede, which I said I would. Oh, and one more thing, he said. "Mark, I want you to be there." Again, I tried to back out, but he wouldn't hear of it. So, several weeks later, the three of us sat down for lunch at the Campus Crusade complex on Lake Hart. True to considerate form, Bright had asked in advance if the rabbi had any dietary concerns.

"As I made my way to his office, I wasn't sure what to expect, as my only real interaction with Campus Crusade for Christ had been at college, which was a less than positive experience," Engel recalled. "But from the first moment I met Dr. Bright I must say that I was drawn in. He was warm, gracious, engaging in a quiet way, and I felt he was genuinely interested in me and my community."

As if, as a journalist, I was not already into this encounter much deeper than I should have been, Bright then turned to me to say the grace. Now, grace before meals is another tricky issue for religion reporters, who frequently dine with clergy. I take ministers to lunch all the time and, as a courtesy, ask if they would like to say grace. What I have found curious is that the evangelical pastors, more than the mainline ministers, are likely to pray with some deference to my own faith, referring to Jesus rather than explicitly using his name in the prayer. Never certain what is coming, I don't usually bow my head or say amen. The lunch with Bright and Engel was the first time I had the tables turned on me. So I offered the grace we have always used at the Brown-Pinsky table, which dates from the time when ours was a religiously mixed marriage. I said the traditional "motzie" blessing in Hebrew, followed by a shaky singing of the Girl Scout grace, "For Health and Strength," that my wife grew up with. After that, I decided I would shut up and see what would happen next. What followed, a discussion between two men of faith, more than forty years apart in age, was fascinating.

"I was interested in his wisdom about building institutions and a vision," Engel said of his host, then more than eighty years old.

> However, Dr. Bright was interested in something else: He wanted to create a relationship, a bridge between his community and mine. I had heard this before, but here the motive was surprisingly different. He had great respect for my tradition, and he was willing to let it stand beside his, without judgment and without wanting to convert me. Dr. Bright had a way of being true and unwavering in his own theology and faith in his Christianity, while at the same time leaving enough room for other's beliefs. This I thought was a rarity in the world in which he so often moved.

Bright then told Engel that he was frequently asked to pray at public events around the country. The Christian wanted to know from the Jew if there was a way to work out wording for such a prayer that would not deny his own beliefs, but would not at the same time offend Jews. I knew from personal experience that this was indeed possible, using terms like "Our Father," "Our God," or "We ask this in your name." A Campus Crusade staff member, Dan Hardaway, is a neighbor and friend of mine, and when our sons were in the same Scout group, I had heard him lead just such a prayer for a gathering that included Christians and Jews. But I was determined to stay out of the conversation. For about fifteen minutes the two men went back and forth until they agreed on a formulation. "He wanted to make sure that it would be a prayer that we could say together, that was faithful to both our traditions," Engel said. "Not a generic prayer that was supposed to not offend anyone and that meant nothing, but a genuine prayer that could meet each of our spiritual needs. This was an amazing aspect to Dr. Bright, being true to his own faith and at the same time allowing others to do the same."

By the end of the lunch, it was clear that a lasting bond had formed between them. Years later, when Bright was near death from pulmonary fibrosis, breathing oxygen from a tank, he called me and asked if I would arrange another meeting with Engel, at his condo. Oh, he added, I want you to be there as well. Saying no to Bright under those circumstances was impossible. What I remember from that day was that, toward the end of the meeting, Bright asked Engel if he would pray for him. "I felt honored to do so," Engel said. The two men stood up, and the rabbi put his arm around Bright, who grabbed me and threw his arm around my shoulder. "We prayed for Shalom, for peace for his body and his soul," the rabbi recalled. "Through his influence I made sure that it could be true to both of our traditions. Though he was ill, that aura of gentle strength and embracing love shone through as we prayed together."

Churchgoing has become a regular part of my reporting on the religion beat. I will drop in on Friday afternoon Juma prayers at local mosques and have come to enjoy the Muslim services. On the other hand, I have about given up on numerous prayer breakfasts in central Florida. It's not so much because they are so early in the morning as much as it is that they are so narrowly focused. Generally, the evangelical organizers do not invite Muslims, Jews, Hindus, Buddhists, or even mainline Protestant clergy. There is a certain smugness to these events I cannot bear. Sunday church services are a different matter. I cannot say that I am ever completely comfortable, but I have relaxed a good bit over the years. In the beginning, I had some primal fear that a passionate pastor might cause me to run screaming down the aisle to the altar to renounce my faith. On other occasions, I felt that if I heard one more word about Jesus, I would run screaming *from* the sanctuary and out the front door. Nowadays, I'm more concerned that I won't have anything smaller than a five-dollar bill in my wallet when they pass the collection plate. If it looks like I'm in one of those hand-holding or hugging congregations, I try to edge away from the nearest person in the pew before it's too late. And I just shake hands when "The peace of the Lord" is exchanged. A byproduct of this churchgoing is that I have become a connoisseur of good preaching. For such a rational person, I confess a weakness for emotional sermons and ecstatic worship. I think that people's weekday, workday lives are so competitive, dulling, and draining that, when Sunday comes, they want to be transported from their earthly lives, if only for an hour or two. So, yes, I do like black churches and small, rural white ones. At one especially moving African American service the congregation was so fervent, I thought for an instant that this is what it must have been like to stand in the crowd at the foot of Mount Sinai when Moses came down. In general, the pews rock and the sermons soar—but not always. The worst sermon I have ever sat through was one Palm Sunday when the African American preacher spoke for more than an hour about blood, sacred and sacrificial, without a hint of joy. And when you are the only white person in the church, there is no unobtrusive way to slip out. As in much of the Sunbelt, the religious landscape in central Florida is changing, sometimes dramatically. True, the area is still overwhelmingly U.S.–born, white, English-speaking, and Christian. That said, there are growing numbers of Jews, Muslims, Hindus, Buddhists, Spanish speakers, and immigrants from around the world. On my beat, I try to capture and cover as much of this diversity as I can. I have also developed a strong interest in the intersection of religion and popular culture (two books and counting), since that approach seems to be successful in drawing nonreligious readers to stories about religion that, frankly, can be a tough sell in a superficial media environment that caters to readers' increasingly short attention span. Still, the biggest sustained religion story for me over the last ten years—locally, regionally, and nationally—has been the rise of American evangelicals. When I came to central Florida and the *Sentinel* in the mid-1990s, I was convinced the movement had peaked and was largely a spent force. That view, as we say in journalism, was "overtaken by events." One of the first of these events was the economic boycott of the Walt Disney Co. by a group of conservative religious groups, including the American Family Association, the Catholic League for Religious and Civil Rights, and the Assemblies of God, a Pentecostal denomination. But the most prominent group in the boycott effort was the Southern Baptist Convention, the nation's largest Protestant denomination. That story, which I have recounted in detail in *The Gospel according to Disney: Faith, Trust, and Pixie Dust* (Westminster John Knox, 2004), involved central Florida's largest employer and the church with the area's greatest number of adherents. As if that were not enough to keep the story on the *Sentinel*'s front page, the president of the Southern Baptist Convention at that time was also the pastor of one of Orlando's largest congregations, First Baptist Church, Rev. Jim Henry.

Religious conservatives felt that Disney, under the leadership of Michael Eisner and Jeffrey Katzenberg, both Jews, had betrayed Uncle Walt's family values tradition. They objected to various company policies and products, including support for health benefits for partners of same-sex employees; facilitating "Gay Days" at the theme parks; and controversial books, movies, and programming on Disney-owned ABC-TV. Although he agreed with many of these complaints, Henry opposed the boycott. There was an element of self-interest in his position, as the minister acknowledged at the time. A number of members of his megachurch worked at Disney and, in their quiet way, were engaging in Christian ministry on the property. But Henry, who was in a distinct minority in his denomination, had another practical reason for his opposition. He believed, correctly as it turns out, that if the Southern Baptist Convention led a Disney boycott and it failed—which it did—it would be difficult for the denomination to be taken seriously again as an economic or political force.

The boycott story had one side benefit, however—bringing me into a close working relationship with Henry. I can still remember our first meeting in his study before the boycott surfaced. In many ways it was a typical meeting between a Jewish reporter raised in the Northeast and a Southern Baptist. He jokingly asked me if, as a Jew, I blamed all Christians for the Inquisition. Because it happened before the Reformation, he felt that Protestants were off the hook for that one. I said there were no hard feelings, since, in any case, Jews did not believe that the sins of the parents were passed on to their descendants, that we'd had a bad experience in that regard. Then it was my turn to ask him what we Jews call the "good German" question. As a southerner, how did he act as a young minister in Mississippi during the turbulent civil rights movement of the 1960s? This was a period in American history when "fine Christian gentleman" was "code in the South for 'segregationist,'" as Diane McWhorter, author of *Carry Me Home: Birmingham, Alabama, the Climactic Battle of the Civil Rights Revolution,* wrote in the August 15, 2005, issue of *The Nation.* While not a racist, Henry conceded he had not done nearly enough in the face of perhaps the greatest moral issue encountered by America in the twentieth century. Henry, a compact, engaging man, had another request for me. He said that conservative Baptists like himself felt that the term "fundamentalist" had become pejorative and marginalizing. I told him that I tend to let people call themselves what they liked, so long as it wasn't "the one true faith," so I would try to avoid the term "fundamentalist" unless it was part of a quotation. (I also tend to eschew the label "ultra-Orthodox" with Jews, or "ultra" anything, since it is often a matter of opinion. Similarly, I ignore evangelicals when they try to convince me that Mormons aren't really Christians.) With that exchange, we were off to a great relationship that endures to this day.

In the evangelical world, megachurch mandarins like Henry are midway between the cable television "leaders" and the grass roots. Keeping in touch with them is valuable. But it was my interactions with evangelical friends and neighbors, as much as my reporting in the office and on the road, that transformed the way I approached my beat. As a result, I discarded the traditional way of structuring my *Orlando Sentinel* stories. No more, "While some wacko evangelical leaders over here say this, these rational secularists and moderate mainliners over there say that," with an author or academic in the middle tossed in for balance. Although symmetrical, this approach is so schematic that it makes the result predictable and unrevealing. On most of these issues, I knew exactly what groups I respect (and often agree with), such as People for the American Way and Americans United for the Separation of Church and State, would say. So instead, I decided to adjust the parameters of my coverage whenever I could, to treat evangelicals as a discrete universe. I started to write about them in a way that would be interesting and informative to my suburban Sunbelt readers—and to me: that is, "Some evangelicals say this, but others disagree," and why and what that means. Once I applied this new template, my stories changed, illuminating fissures and fault lines within the evangelical movement and, I hope, adding to the general knowledge. As John Wilson, editor of the intellectual journal *Books & Culture: A Christian Review,* told Peter Steinfels of the *New York Times* on September 3, 2005, the evangelical world is "much more diverse and less predictable on the inside than it looks on the outside." Still, not everyone among *Sentinel* readers was happy with this approach. Members of liberal and moderate mainline denominations wrote or called—mostly in good spirit—that they felt I was giving short shrift to the millions of more progressive Christians. While in many ways my heart was with them, the membership of mainline denominations is steadily shrinking, and they are losing influence on both the local and national level. As observers as disparate as Rick Warren and Martin Marty have pointed out, increasingly "mainline" means "sideline" when it comes to

American Protestant denominations. The dynamism in the Sunbelt was—and is—with the evangelicals. Why this is true is not entirely clear to me. It may be, as some evangelical leaders and thinkers argue, the comfort of orthodox theology, conservative values, and clearly defined gender roles in uncertain times.

While covering the Disney boycott, I sensed—as Jews often do, sometimes without reason—a strong subtext of anti-Semitism among those attacking the entertainment giant. That is, these two Jewish Philistines or Pharisees (Eisner and Katzenberg) have ruined what Walt Disney, a WASP icon if there ever was one, took a lifetime to create. Somewhere between prejudice and paranoia, whenever they said "Hollywood," I heard "Jews." I never heard those words explicitly, and I couldn't document the feeling, so I never wrote it. For a reporter, a downside of people knowing I was Jewish was that it was unlikely they would make anti-Semitic remarks in my presence. I think the same thing was true when I attended Muslim gatherings, where I know feelings against Israel must run quite high. And to be honest, in informal settings I frequently hear my fellow Jews make incredibly racist and categorical remarks about Arabs and Muslims. This "internal dialogue," based on shared assumptions (and prejudices) and conducted behind closed doors, rarely appears in print. But sometimes the veil slips, and when it does and we report it, the internal dialogue can enter the "external conversation." Statements and sentiments that are accepted and considered normal within the group can cause acute embarrassment when published or broadcast throughout the nation.

At the annual Southern Baptist Conventions and pastors' conferences, I have heard a fair amount of anti-Catholic and anti-Muslim rhetoric, which I have written about. Protestants make common cause with Catholics on issues like abortion—an alliance the Southern Baptist Convention's Richard Land calls "the liberals' worst nightmare"—gay marriage, euthanasia, and stem-cell research. But fellow Southern Baptist leaders like Reverend Albert Mohler regularly appear on the *Larry King Show,* where they describe Catholicism as a "cult." A Mississippi pro-life group, Bethany Christian Services, which received money from the state's "Choose Life" license plates, acknowledged that it would not place adoptees with Roman Catholic families, because their faith conflicted with the organization's Statement of Faith. (The adoption agency's national leadership reversed the decision after this was reported by the Associated Press.) Billy Graham's son and ministry heir, Franklin Graham, is notorious for his derogatory comments about non-Christian groups, referring to Hindus as "pagans," for example.

Rev. Paige Patterson, president of Southeastern Baptist Theological Seminary, a former president of the denomination, frequently boasted, "I do not have an ecumenical bone in my body." In the wake of the 9/11 bombings and national trauma, I wrote about a number of interfaith and interdenominational prayer gatherings. In the course of reporting on these efforts, I noted that Southern Baptists, our largest denomination, would not be participating because their practice (like that of some others, including Missouri Synod Lutherans and some Orthodox Jewish clergy) is not to pray publicly with those who do not share their basic theology. This fact struck a nerve, as far away as Nashville, headquarters of the Southern Baptist Convention. Southern Baptists did not deny that this was the case; they simply objected that I had reported it.

My role as religion writer sometimes puts me in an odd position. Every so often someone will call me about a book or a ministry or simply a message that they are certain will lead to world salvation, if only I can help get this news out. I try to listen patiently and politely for as long as I can. Then I say something like this: I'm not qualified to judge theology, so I don't do stories like this. However, I am certain that if the Lord wants this message to reach the ears of the people who need to hear it, he'll find a way. It's a device, but it usually works.

There are other constants to the religion beat. Every congregation I encounter says it is growing, and just about every religious leader I meet is convinced we are in revival. This kind of predictable thinking is not confined to the people I write about; it includes the people I work for. Invariably, when a natural disaster or accident or horrific crime takes place in our circulation area—usually a hurricane or a tornado—I am dispatched to houses of worship to ask the faithful and their pastoral leaders how they think God could allow something like this to happen. Not only are my marching orders the same; these stories are all the same and arrive at the same conclusion: God does not cause accidents or disasters or evil; believers' faith remains strong. Every time.

I am particularly sensitive about the coverage I give to my own faith, Judaism. An accepted convention among religion writers is that you do not write about your own congregation if there is any way to avoid doing so. I imagine there is some kvetching among my friends in my synagogue, now renamed the Congregation of Reform Judaism, over this policy, but I try to abide by it. I quote my rabbi, Steve Engel, when doing roundup stories or when he serves as chairman of the Greater Orlando Board of Rabbis, or when I can't reach any of the other rabbis on deadline. Because I am vulnerable to criticism that I cover my own faith disproportionately, or that I favor it over Christianity (the Muslims have never complained), I probably set the bar higher than necessary for stories about Judaism, which may cause additional muttering among co-religionists pitching me stories. I have made certain concessions to my faith, stylistic compromises in my coverage. On the one hand, I don't use the word "Christ," which means Messiah, unless it is part of a quote, a title, or the name of an organization; I stick with "Jesus," at least in that sense. On the other hand, in dating historical events I use "B.C.," "Before Christ," rather than the more awkward and (in Central Florida) more confusing "B.C.E.," "Before the Common Era." For the same reasons of convenience, I use "Old Testament" rather than "Hebrew Bible," a formulation many Jews and progressive Christians prefer.

One of the most difficult challenges I have faced has been dealing with those who call themselves "Messianic Jews." In general, I shy away from conversion stories of any kind. They're like stories about happy second marriages: you can't really talk about the new one that has brought such happiness without dealing with the one that didn't work out. The fact that, with Messianics, the "first wife" was Judaism was hard for me. In writing such stories, I don't use the term "completed Jew," which some converts prefer, any more than I would use a term like "recovering Baptist" or "recovering Catholic," and for the same reason—they are inherently gratuitous. To complicate matters for me, a growing number of local national evangelical leaders I interviewed or wrote about were born Jewish: Rev. Marvin Rosenthal, founder of Orlando's Holy Land Experience; attorney Jay Sekulow, founder of the American Center for Law and Justice; Christian fitness guru Jordan Rubin, author of *The Maker's Diet*; Marvin Olasky, founder of *World* magazine; Rev. Louis Sheldon, founder of the Traditional Values Coalition.

I am not alone in wrestling with this issue. Members of the Religion Newswriters Association's Listserv—Jews, Gentiles, and at least one Messianic reporter—also struggle. Jeff Weiss, my colleague at the *Dallas Morning News,* who is also Jewish, learned that a Messianic congregation in his city planned to display an Israeli bus that had been blown up by Palestinian terrorists on Yom Kippur, the Day of Atonement, in 2004. "I immediately called several local Jewish leaders," he wrote on the Religion Newswriters Association Web site. "I was careful in my conversation to say explicitly that I wasn't looking to make news, wasn't looking to create reaction. But if they had one, I wanted to know about it. And some of them did. And we put it in the paper." Debate on the subject of whether Messianics are Jews got so heated that moderators felt they had to cut it off.

The issues raised by the Messianics were tenacious—and recurring. Early in my tenure as religion writer, local rabbis called me to complain about the *Sentinel*'s Saturday "faith calendar," a paid advertising grid that lists the names, addresses, and service times of houses of worship, by denomination, for a small fee. Messianics were listed under "Jewish," which was driving community leaders nuts. I suggested they go over my head with the complaint, and ultimately the Messianics got their own separate denominational listing. Later, in May 1997, a coalition of evangelical churches in central Florida sponsored a candle-lighting memorial for the Holocaust, advertised as a "United Christian Witness to the Jews of Orlando." The gathering was held in the tourist area, at a hotel owned by Harris Rosen, a prominent member of the Jewish community, and implied that there would be Jewish participation. In fact, the only Jews involved were Jewish converts actively proselytizing. Worse, the event was scheduled at the exact same time as the official and long-standing ecumenical Yom HaShoah observation at the other end of the county, putting the two observations in direct competition. Michael Nebel, an Orlando attorney and former president of the Holocaust Memorial Research and Education Center of Central

Florida, the sponsor of the annual event, called the competing gathering "unbelievable. I am deeply offended."

On the international front, Messianics and their evangelical supporters complicate the issue of conservative Christian support for Israel, a movement loosely known as Christian Zionism. This unquestioning evangelical support for the Israeli government stands in increasingly marked contrast with critical stands taken by mainline denominations like the Presbyterian Church (U.S.A.) and the United Church of Christ on Israeli policy in the Occupied Territories. In 1998, a five-day national conference of evangelicals called "Israel's Jubilee," marking the state's fiftieth anniversary, raised similar concerns. Prominent among the participants were Messianics, which caused most invited rabbis to stay away. In response to the ensuing controversy, proselytizing among the thousands at the gathering was hastily banned by the sponsoring group, Jacksonville-based Christian Alliance for Israel. Even for as staunch a supporter of Jewish-evangelical cooperation as Rabbi Eckstein, who opposed the Southern Baptist conversion effort, and who told the *New York Times* magazine in July of 2005 that "Jews tend to demonize evangelicals," this was also too much. The only rabbi who showed up was Rabbi Daniel Lapin, a Seattle radio host and founder of the conservative organization Toward Tradition, who brushed aside other rabbis' concerns, saying, "Observant and believing Jews do not become Christians." Lapin did not address another reason for evangelical support of Israel: for some, the final ingathering of the Jews to a resurgent Israel is the theological prerequisite for Jesus' second coming. Of course they believe but do not say that when that happens, those of us who do not convert to Christianity will die and burn in hell's fiery lake for a thousand years.

As recently as November of 2005, the Jewish community of central Florida confronted a dilemma. A local evangelical group, led by *Charisma* magazine founder Steve Strang, called a rally for Christian support of Israel, featuring Rev. John Hagee of Texas. The goal was to raise enough money to purchase an ambulance for Magen David Adom, the Israeli affiliate of the International Red Cross. Local rabbis were invited to be on hand when the check was presented to a representative of the Israeli government. Some rabbis, like Aaron Rubinger, agreed to participate after stating their concerns about proselytizing. Strang, the Christian publishing mogul, told me that he had assured the rabbis that, if they showed up, the Messianics would "behave themselves" at the event.

A local Jewish leader, David Bornstein, opposed Jewish participation in the meeting, in the October 28, 2005, issue of the *Heritage* Jewish weekly newspaper. "The issue about how Jews and evangelicals relate is a perplexing one," he wrote.

On the one hand, we are and have been fertile territory for conversion, lest our souls, in the minds of the Christian right, be damned for eternity. On the other hand, the existence of Israel and the return of Jews from the Diaspora is a signal to many of the coming rapture, which is, after all, what many fundamentalist Christians look forward to. Without us, their salvation may not occur. On that basis they love Israel and support her with cash and tourism. Sounds like we should be right there along with them, right? Unfortunately, it's not that simple. . . . Dr. Hagee appears, on the surface, to be the kind of devout Christian we could proudly call friend. Unfortunately, this ignores his stand on many other issues, including but not limited to gay rights, civil rights, women's rights, abortion, prayer in the public schools, and many others. Are we willing to leap into partnership with someone who shares our love for Israel, but diverges with so many of us on so many other important issues? And of course we must acknowledge that the vast majority of fundamentalist Christians proselytize and attempt to convert as a foundation of their beliefs. Is it all right to support Hagee when he does believe in conversion efforts in the Third World, just because he leaves us alone? I don't think so.

Rubinger replied the next week in the *Heritage,* calling on central Florida's Jews to join him and other leaders at the event

to express a loud and clear "thank you" to those Christians who have remained loyal and vocal advocates of the State of Israel. . . . While we know that Evangelicals, in general, are of the belief that Jews should be converted to Christianity, Pastor John Hagee, the renowned and charismatic minister of the Cornerstone Church of San Antonio, Texas, who will be speaking and conducting this program, has been nationally outspoken as being in opposition to efforts to convert the Jews. For that view, he has been strongly criticized by others of his faith, yet he has remained steadfast in his position.

Rubinger said he had been assured that "no proselytizing activity of any sort" would be permitted at the rally. Strang told the rabbis, Rubinger wrote, that, "Should anyone try to 'hijack' this event, they will be stopped right in their tracks. We will gather together that night solely to demonstrate our support for Israel. There is no hidden agenda."

Strang was as good as his word. More than a thousand people showed up at the Altamonte Springs Hilton for the rally, including at least two hundred Jews. In the packed hotel ballroom I noticed my cousin Bea Sherzer, in a row of Temple Israel synagogue members. She motioned me to an empty seat next to her, so I joined her. At first, Bea—who is in her eighties—and her friends seemed uncomfortable to be among so many singing, dancing, hand-waving Pentecostals. A few may have feared a pogrom might break out. But after a DVD featuring a blazing country-and-western version of "Hava Nagila," recorded at Hagee's church, was projected onto a screen, and Hagee launched into his speech, the Jews lost their inhibitions and got revved up, too, applauding and jumping to their feet.

Four rabbis attended, delivering both the invocation and the benediction. Jesus' name was barely heard, and there were no Messianics on the dais, although there were some in the crowd. Hagee's rousing "speech" sounded as though he was running for prime minister of Israel. "Hagee spoke like Menachem Begin, only with a Texas accent!" Rubinger told his congregation in a sermon after the rally. The evangelist reminded Christians in the audience that the Jews were the "apple of God's eye," that those who blessed them would be blessed, and those who cursed them would be cursed. "Look at the names of the prophets in the Bible," he exhorted. "Notice they are all, without exception, *Jewish* names—*not a single Southern Baptist name amongst them!*" Just under $120,000 was raised for "an emergency room on wheels."

Only one rabbi from a major area congregation, Steve Engel, of the Congregation of Reform Judaism, did not appear. "I didn't go because I had some concerns about the motivation behind the support for Israel," he said. The Reform rabbi applauded the rally's backing of the Jewish state, but he was cautious because of the association of some Christian Zionists with some "end times" theology that says the in-gathering of the Jews in Israel is a prerequisite for Jesus' second coming. "It's hard for me to accept one part of the package without accepting the whole package," Engel said. But Engel's and Bornstein's position was supported on the national level in speeches by Rabbi Eric Yoffie, head of the Reform movement, and by Abraham Foxman of the Anti-Defamation League, who noted the evangelicals' views on abortion, stem-cell research, the role of women, and, most critically, the separation of church and state. Foxman told a meeting of the ADL's National Commission on November 3, 2005, that the religious right presented "the key domestic challenge to the American Jewish community and to our democratic values. . . . What we're seeing is a pervasive, intensive assault on the traditional balance between religion and state in this country. . . . They're not . . . talking about God and religious values, but about Jesus and Christian values." The goal of these interest groups is nothing less than "Christianizing America," Foxman charged. "We are facing an emerging Christian Right leadership that intends to 'Christianize' all aspects of American life," Foxman said, "from the halls of government to the libraries, to the movies, to recording studios, to the playing fields and locker rooms of professional, collegiate, and amateur sports, from the military to SpongeBob SquarePants."

"What could be more bigoted than to claim that you have a monopoly on God?" Yoffie asked members of his 1.5-million-member denomination at their biennial convention in Houston on November 19, 2005. "Yes, we can disagree about gay marriage. But there is no excuse for hateful rhetoric that fuels the hellfires of antigay bigotry." When conservatives "cloak themselves in religion and forget mercy, it strikes us as blasphemy," Yoffie said. "We need beware the zealots who want to make their religion the religion of everyone else. We are particularly offended by the suggestion that the opposite of the religious right is the voice of atheism. We are appalled when 'people of faith' is used in such a way that it excludes us, as well as most Jews, Catholics, and Muslims. What could be more bigoted than to claim that you have a monopoly on God and that anyone who disagrees with you is not a person of faith?"

Mark Silk, director of the Leonard E. Greenberg Center for the Study of Religion in Public Life at Trinity College in Hartford, Connecticut, put the Foxman and Yoffie speeches in perspective. "What evangelicals don't seem to understand is that when Christians are on the march, Jews tend to run the other way," he told Paul Nussbaum of the *Philadelphia Inquirer*. "I fail to see much prospect of a new entente." Another thing some evangelicals don't understand is that—with the possible (and occasional) exception of the Israeli army—Jews do not march in lockstep anymore than Christians do. Thus, some Christian right leaders reacted to the Foxman and Yoffie speeches by muttering darkly that Jewish supporters of Israel who value Christian backing on that issue might do well to keep their leaders in line.

Rabbi James Rudin of the American Jewish Committee seemed to take a middle view when I asked him about the debate over accepting evangelical support for Israel. "The question is: 'What is the price?' The Jewish people, like all people, have no permanent friends. We have permanent interests. The interest of the Jewish people is survival of Israel and the survival of the Jewish people." Working with mainline Christians, some of whom "support us on domestic issues, but are critical or even hostile to Israel's existence," is equally problematic, said Rudin, author of *The Baptizing of America: The Religious Right's Plans for the Rest of Us.*

> But I think we have to work with mainline Christian leaders on domestic issues. We may disagree with the evangelicals on those same domestic issues, but they are very strong with us on support for survival and security of Israel. I think it's "both/and." Often we get evangelical support for Israel but not an evangelical understanding of Judaism. The key thing is, they can't hold up a sign that says "Modern Israel, yes, but Judaism, no."

My coverage of the Hagee rally for the *Sentinel* was illustrative of how impossible it to satisfy partisans when reporting on issues involving the Middle East. A news story about the rally, written for the next day's paper, would have had to be a short one in the local section, without any photographs, given the late timing of the Altamonte gathering, and the newspaper's deadlines. That kind of short-shrift, "quick-and-dirty" story would no doubt have provoked cries of outrage. So my editors and I decided to wait and explore the larger issue of Christian Zionism in a subsequent feature story. Other breaking news intervened, and then the Christmas and Hanukkah season loomed. It was January before we could get the story into the paper, but in this case timing worked in our favor. The issue of Christians and Jews and Israel was emerging; with stories in the *Washington Post* and *Philadelphia Inquirer*, the Foxman and Yoffie speeches got national coverage, and then came Pat Robertson's tone-deaf comments about Israeli Prime Minister Ariel Sharon's stroke. When my story finally appeared, it began with the Florida rally, but in fairness to all sides, I also recounted the division within the Jewish community, locally and nationally, on the issue of Christian Zionism. I also included brief comments by an American Muslim spokesman, a Palestinian Catholic, and a Palestinian-American Protestant, Rev. Fahed Abu-Fakel. I thought Abu-Fakel was critical, since he was a former national leader of the Presbyterian Church (U.S.A.), a denomination that had recently been critical of Israeli policy in the Occupied Territories. Abu-Fakel called Christian Zionism "racist, destructive, and unbiblical," leaving Palestinian Christians feeling "abandoned and forgotten." Not surprisingly, my story drew spirited and strenuous criticism from both *Charisma*'s Strang and Rabbi Rubinger. Their objections, voiced to the *Sentinel*'s reader representative Manning Pynn, were that the rally and its significance formed too small a part in my story, and that the larger issues I discussed were essentially irrelevant. The issue of who in the Israel/Palestine dispute had a divine—and thus superior—claim on the land did not seem to them one that had two legitimate sides.

As a Jew covering religion, I was surprised to find intense competition, even cattiness, among Christians—although in retrospect I don't know why. Whenever I hear someone say, "He's a good Christian," I am certain that the next thing I hear will sound like a verbal knife slipped between the shoulder blades. On the basketball court, you are as likely to see sharp elbows and hip checks when Christians play as when non-Christians play. On October 28, 2005, the founder, principal, and football coach of Texas Christian School, a Houston area high school, told his team members their game was cancelled, and ordered them to turn in their uniforms for "inspection." Herc Palmquist, who is also a Bible-study teacher at the school he owns, then recruited college-aged "ringers" to play as the team instead. TCS lost anyway, 28-18, and when news leaked out, he was suspended for five games by the Texas Association of Private and Parochial Schools. "I believe those who know me and know me well know that I would never intentionally hurt my savior, my family, TCS or any team," Palmquist wrote in a letter of apology to the association, according to the November 17, 2005, *Houston Chronicle*.

In religion, as on any beat, some of the greatest stories never get into the paper. In the 1980s, I was researching a series of investigative stories on religious television for the *Los Angeles Times*. I found a man, then working in Christian media in northern California, who told me the following story about two of the most famous (if overly made-up and hair-sprayed) women televangelists of the era. Ten years before, they and their husbands—one of whom would later go to federal prison and one who would go on to become the Citizen Kane of Christian broadcasting—were partners in a struggling Orange County UHF television station. Late one night, my informant told me, he was working at the station when he heard a terrible racket in the hallway. There he saw the two wives in a knockdown, drag-out, screaming fistfight. "Each was accusing the other of being demon-possessed," he recalled with a chuckle. "And I was inclined to believe both of them." Alas, my source would not let me quote him by name, so until now the anecdote has remained unpublished. Enjoy. If you can't figure out who is who, I won't help you.

Holy warriors indeed. Sometimes such combative fervor spills into other, more substantive arenas—political, educational, and judicial.

Chapter 4

Warriors, Holy and Unholy

Who's Pushing Whom?

*O*n June 20, 2005, on the floor of the U.S. House of Representatives, Congressman David Obey proposed an amendment to the budget for the U.S. Air Force Academy condemning "coercive and abusive religious proselytizing" at the Colorado university. The Wisconsin Democrat was reacting to charges that evangelicals on the faculty and staff, as well as in the student body, had acted inappropriately and in a discriminatory way toward nonevangelicals, including Jewish students. Debate over the amendment, which was ultimately defeated 210-198 on a party-line vote, drew these remarks from Republican Congressman John Hostettler of Indiana: "The long war on Christianity in America continues today on the floor of the House of Representatives, and continues unabated with aid and comfort to those who would eradicate any vestige of our Christian heritage being supplied by the usual suspects, the Democrats." He added, "Like a moth to a flame, Democrats can't help themselves when it comes to denigrating and demonizing Christians."

Apoplectic, Obey took the floor and protested the remarks, which Hostettler agreed to withdraw, at least in part. But the exchange was catnip to Jon Stewart, of Comedy Central's *The Daily Show*. On the show that aired June 22, 2005, the host introduced an item on what he called "America's most important reality show: Congress. What happens when they stop being nice and start using hyperbolic rhetoric?" After playing clips of Hostettler's diatribe, Stewart—who is Jewish—said, his voice dripping with sarcasm, "Yes, the long war on Christianity. I pray that one day we may live in an America where

Christians can worship freely! In broad daylight! Openly wearing the symbols of their religion . . . perhaps around their necks?" Alternately pleading and rolling his eyes, Stewart continued, "And maybe—dare I dream it?—maybe one day there can be an openly Christian President. Or, perhaps, forty-three of them. Consecutively." Several nights later, Stewart returned to the subject. "Does anyone know—does the Christian persecution complex have an expiration date? Because, ahh, you've been in charge pretty much since, ahh, what was that guy's name—Constantine? . . . I'm just saying, enjoy your success."

Without question, we as Americans have been engaged in a great, sometimes uncivil war over culture, faith, and moral values for at least twenty-five years—although the conflict has waxed and waned during that period. So, in this dispute who is pushing whom? What kind of a conflict is it when *both* sides say they are being attacked and claim to be on the defensive, the victims of intolerance and, in some cases, even persecution? The answer is complicated. "There is a great deal of anxiety, whether it's among secularists or Jews or Roman Catholics or evangelicals, about whether their values will be respected and whether they will ultimately prevail," John C. Green of the Pew Center told *Fortune* magazine on October 31, 2005. "Everyone feels beleaguered and persecuted. And with some justification." A national survey conducted November 19–21, 2004, by Gallup for *USA Today* and CNN found that 48 percent of Americans say that religion has too much influence in American life, while 40 percent say it has too little. A Pew Center poll released in July of 2005 found that 45 percent of Americans thought conservatives have gone too far in trying to impose their religious values on the country, while an equal percentage disagreed. In a nationwide poll of eight hundred adults, released November 21, 2005, 64 percent agreed that "religion is under attack" in the United States (80 percent of those identifying themselves as evangelical/fundamental/charismatic Christians agreed with the statement). But 45 percent of those in the poll, "American Attitudes toward Religion in the Public Square," commissioned by the Anti-Defamation League and conducted by the Marttila Communications Group, also agreed with the statement that "right wing religious leaders are seeking to impose their religious beliefs on everyone else." A *Los Angeles Times* nationwide poll of 1,033 adults, conducted January 15–17, 2005, by the Roper Center for Public Opinion Research, found that 44 percent of those surveyed thought the separation of church and state was very important, with another 24 percent saying it was somewhat important. Each side has complaints—some lurid, some ludicrous, and some valid.

Examined closely, the fundamental dispute between these two Americas is not so much centered on laws and policy, although these are frequently the battlegrounds. Rather, it is about what represents society's ideal, and the ability of one side or the other to advance that ideal. Is it heterosexual marriage? Is it a diverse and multicultural society? In the Sunbelt and some southern midwest, Rocky Mountain, and plains states areas of evangelical strength, and in rural areas generally, more conservative attitudes regarding education—prayer in public schools and the teaching of creationism—morality, and abortion prevail. There, public expressions of Christianity in courtrooms and city squares are enforced through public opinion, individual action, and the ballot box. So it is not surprising that people in these areas who hold minority views sometimes feel intimidated by the majority. They believe they are being pressured in this environment to conform to values they do not share, and in extreme cases they may generalize their local situation. That is, some may feel religious conservatives are throwing their weight around while, conversely and simultaneously, Christians in secular strongholds around the country may feel they are being discriminated against.

In the summer of 2005, for example, the Tulsa, Oklahoma, Zoo—one of nine "living zoos" in the United States—decided it wasn't such a good idea after all to mount a Genesis exhibition, telling the story of biblical creation, in order to balance an evolution science exhibit. One speaker at a city board meeting, Dan Hicks, said the display was necessary to counter other religious symbols at the zoo, including a stone sculpture of elephant-head Hindu deity Ganesh, which he called an affront to the area's Christian population. Creationism, as we will see, simply does not have traction among suburban evangelicals. Similarly, and in contrast to an issue like public financial support for religious schools (particularly vouchers), draping classic nude sculpture is not a middle-class issue for evangelicals. When U.S. Attorney General John Ashcroft had a partially clothed statue of a woman in the Justice Department's lobby covered up for a press conference, the episode drew national attention only because it was in Washington, D.C., in the glare of television lights. In the Sunbelt, outcries about such coverups, which frequently seem to involve displays of Michelangelo's *David,* happen often enough to be of marginal news value. The proprietors of Rainbow City, a gay-oriented business in Orlando, had to cover their copy of the statue after a complaint about nudity to city officials. In 1996, the principal at Dillard High School in Fort Lauderdale threw a tarp over a student's larger-than-life sculpture of a nude man in the lobby of the school's performing arts building.

In December of 2005 the superintendent of schools in Fulton, Missouri, received three complaints from members of Calloway Christian Church about an expurgated version of the 1950s-era musical *Grease* that had been performed the month before by students at Fulton High School. As a result of the complaints, the official, Mark Enderle, pulled the plug on the upcoming spring production of Arthur Miller's *The Crucible,* telling the *New York Times* he banned the drama, which he called "a fine play," to prevent the school from being "mired in controversy."

On March 19, 2005, the *New York Times* reported that creationists—or the fear of them—in a dozen southern cities blocked showings of the 2003 IMAX movie *Volcanoes of the Deep Sea,* because they said it contradicted the biblical account of Genesis. Among those rejecting the $8 million big-screen film, which was sponsored by the National Science Foundation and Rutgers University, were a number of Sunbelt science centers. Carol Murray, director of marketing for the Fort Worth Museum of Science and History, told the *Times* that, following a preview screening, "some people said it was blasphemous." Lisa Buzzelli, director of the Charleston IMAX theater, located next to the city's aquarium, attributed her decision to the fact that Charleston, being in the Bible Belt, "we have definitely a lot more [of a] creation public than evolution public."

How evolution is presented in the public schools is another hot-button issue that skews along class lines among evangelicals. Yes, at least nineteen states—many but not all in the Sunbelt—are considering proposals dealing with the issue of how to teach evolution. Evangelical activists say they simply want to note that evolution is not an undisputed fact, but a "theory" of the development of life on earth, and one of several at that. What is ironic—if not disingenuous—to me is that these religious critics use the scientific method to undermine Darwin, a line of attack scientists are bound by their discipline to take seriously. Yet many of these same people and their supporters would never accept the scientific method as a valid challenge to their "young earth" view of biblical creationism, belief in a seven-day creation six thousand years ago. This is a fringe movement inflated by activists, special pleaders, and cable television gasbags. Strictly speaking, gravity and heliocentricity are also "theories."

The Pew Center poll in 2005 found that 70 percent of white evangelical Protestants said that life has existed in its present form since the beginning of time. But at the same time, I have found that creationism, a more fundamentalist and literal belief in the earth's origins, is no longer intellectually acceptable in many Sunbelt suburbs, where parents want their bright children to find places at top state universities, the Ivy League, Duke, and Stanford, not to mention medical school. A similar point was presciently made by one of the antievolution fathers early in the 1960 movie version of *Inherit the Wind*, based on the Scopes monkey trial in Dayton, Tennessee, in 1925. He wonders whether the law will hurt his son's chances to get into Yale. And this is no idle concern. On August 25, 2005, the 800-member Association of Christian Schools International sued the University of California system, charging they do not accept credits for high school science courses based on creationism or challenging Darwin. Thus, suburban parents are unlikely to support proposals to put stickers in their children's high school biology textbooks that read, "There may have been dinosaurs on Noah's ark." Hence the emergence of creationism's more plausible successor, "intelligent design," which allows evangelicals to finesse evidence of Darwinian evolution within species. Arguing that the world is too complex to be entirely random, Intelligent Design advocates say that God may have mapped out all of human creation in advance, or at least hit the switch on the big bang to get everything rolling. In fact, this view is not incompatible with Darwin's own speculation in *Origin of the Species* about a Creator's role in sparking life. Some call it "creationism in a cheap tuxedo," and in Frazier Mountain, California, a rural school district north of Los Angeles, education officials were forced to withdraw an elective course called "Philosophy of Design," after parents—with the help of Americans United for the Separation of Church and State—sued in federal court. But it's not a bad fallback; mainstream Judaism and the Enlightenment deists have essentially taken this view—before it had a name—for hundreds of years. On August 1, 2005, President Bush said in an interview with Texas newspaper reporters that intelligent design should be taught along with evolution in public schools, "so people can understand what the debate is about." Richard Land, of the Southern Baptist Convention, hailed the president's remarks, but Bush's science advisor, John H. Marburger III, got busy backpedaling. "Evolution is the cornerstone of modern biology," he told the *New York Times*. "Intelligent design is not a scientific concept." The president's brother, Florida Governor Jeb Bush, has been a profile in waffling on the issue. He pandered to his lower-middle-class and rural supporters one day, implying support for teaching intelligent design in the state's schools, while excluding Darwin. Then, a few days later, to avoid embarrassing himself with upper-middle-class, suburban parents, he (or one of his aides) said that the public school's science curriculum should be determined "by educators, not politicians."

Nor is opposition to Darwinian evolution a preserve of fundamentalist Christians; a small, Orthodox Jewish group has banned the books of Rabbi Nosson Slifkin for his support of Darwin, according to the October 2005 issue of *Moment* magazine. In 2005, two Orthodox Jewish groups in South Florida organized conferences on intelligent design. William Dembski, of Southern Baptist Theological Seminary, the movement's intellectual founder, was the featured speaker at the International Conference on Torah & Science, held at Florida International University in Miami. Aish Ha-Torah of Hollywood invited Gerald Schroeder, an Israeli-American scholar, to compare intelligent design to Darwinism. "This is a fundamental American issue for anyone who takes God and the Bible seriously," Rabbi Tzvi Nightingale told James D. Davis of the South Florida *Sun-Sentinel*.

After a trial in Dover, Pennsylvania, challenging a local school board decision to acknowledge intelligent design in textbooks, U.S. District Judge John E. Jones III dismissed it as "a mere relabeling of creationism, and not a scientific theory," and "a particular version of Christianity." In his scathing, 139-page decision, Jones called the school board's decision an example of "breathtaking inanity."

Public schools continue to be a battleground for evangelicals, and not just on the subject of evolution. The issue of which books are fit for public schools can cut both ways, geographically. In Lake Wales, Florida, according to reports in the *Orlando Sentinel* and Lakeland, Florida, *Ledger,* the mother of a nine-year-old girl tried to ban six novels written by two-time Newbery Award–winner Lois Lowry from all Polk County elementary school libraries. Kristi Hardee, a part-time church secretary, said her daughter chose to read *Anastasia Krupnik.* When she found some "bad" words in it, she told her teacher, who then told her mother. Hardee called the book "vulgar," and at one point she said she checked it out of the library so no one else could read it (so much for the marketplace of ideas). In February of 2005, Hardee and her supporters, including her father-in-law, the Rev. Kenneth Hardee, of Lake Region Baptist Church, succeeded in getting the book removed from her daughter's Spook Hill Elementary School. The pastor told the school board that, while he realized everyone has rights, "I also realize that within those rights, we as Christians have rights." But the county school board refused to remove the other five books from elementary schools in the county. Jacqueline Rose, the senior coordinator for the county's school library system, opposed any removal, noting that in the previous twenty-four years forty books had been challenged by individual school library committees, and only three had been banned.

Far to the north, on both sides of the Delaware River, Christian parents claimed they were discriminated against in their children's schools. In eastern Pennsylvania, Donna Busch said that other parents in her son's kindergarten class at Culbertson Elementary School were able to read from their children's favorite books during "Me Week." But when her son chose the Bible as his favorite book, Busch was prohibited from reading four verses from the book of Psalms. In Medford, New Jersey, a first-grade student was not permitted to read to his class from *The Beginners Bible.* (The boy's position in that case was supported by a U.S. Circuit Court of Appeals judge named Samuel Alito.) In other cases around the country, students claimed they were not allowed to bring Bibles to school and read them on their own time. Christian legal groups like Liberty Counsel were quick to come to their aid, with frequent success. The issue extends to higher education. Although California State University at San Bernardino allows religious organizations like Hillel, whose membership is limited to Jews, in December of 2005 the school's administration blocked a group of Christian students from forming a campus group because membership would be restricted on the basis of religious beliefs and sexual orientation.

Other issues in Sunbelt schools, where evangelicals are often the overwhelming majority, are more a matter of substance than symbolism. In 1993, in rural Pontotoc, Mississippi, Lisa Herdahl objected to a half-century practice of prayer, Bible study, and other religious activities in the elementary school where three of her six children attended. These included student-led morning prayers over the school's intercom; prayer meetings in the gym; prayers in classes before lunch; and Bible classes led by teachers selected and paid by local churches. Herdahl said that when she objected to school officials, she was rebuffed. One child was given earphones to block the sound, while others were escorted from class during religious activities. With the help of the American Civil Liberties Union and People for the American Way, Herdahl brought suit in federal district court, where in 1996 Judge Neal Biggers Jr. outlawed all of the school district's practices except for voluntary morning prayer in the gym. "The Bill of Rights was created to protect the minority from the tyranny of the majority," he wrote in his decision. The ruling did not protect Herdahl from losing her job, social isolation, and what she said were mailed death threats. The Pontotoc County superintendent of public schools, Jerry Horton, called the ruling "a setback for religious freedom," and Mississippi Republican elected officials denounced the decision. Before the case was decided, more than three thousand local residents rallied at the county courthouse for a "God and Country" rally, an event organized by area church leaders and students.

In middle and high schools in the Sunbelt, Jews and others have complained that assemblies, advisors, and teachers were involved in aggressive, even coercive proselytizing, sometimes resulting in heated confrontations. In extreme cases, youth ministers representing groups like Young Life and Student Venture were invited onto the campus during the school day to evangelize, some roaming the cafeterias in the guise of "counselors." Mandatory assemblies featured evangelical performances by organizations like the Fellowship of Christian Athletes. This atmosphere of religious permissiveness was the result of both lawsuits and governmental guidelines instituted under the Clinton administration. "The result has been the greatest amount of religious expression in public schools in our nation's history," said Jay Sekulow, of the American Center for Law and Justice, a Christian legal group, financed by Pat Robertson, that argued many of the cases. In 1995, officials at Lake Mary High School outside of Orlando received a report that a youth minister from a local church had approached several non-Christian students and used harsh words during his lunchtime evangelism. As a result, the Seminole County school district sharply restricted such visits, issuing a memo that outlined "a far more cautious position regarding equal access" to campuses. In 1996, at nearby Lake Brantley High School in Seminole County, several parents complained that a teacher delivered Christian testimony in class. Students were invited to her home for a voluntary review of class work, after which she would lead a Bible study group. "It wasn't a formal thing," said Ned Julian, attorney for Seminole County schools, "but we suggested to her that you can't do that in your role as public school teacher in a public school classroom, and that was the end of it."

Another touchy situation can occur when teachers and administrators in middle and high schools wear T-shirts in their classes and offices proclaiming Christian faith. At Poinciana High School in Kissimmee, Florida, the principal briefly banned teachers and staff members from wearing T-shirts of the Fellowship of Christian Athletes, a campus club with chapters in nearly eighty central Florida high schools, on Friday "Spirit Days." After negotiations with Liberty Counsel, a Maitland, Florida–based organization much like Sekulow's American Center for Law and Justice, the teachers and administrators were permitted to wear the T-shirts, with "Champions in Christ" on the front and a New Testament verse on the back. Poinciana principal Michael Brizendine issued a memo explaining that the shirts "are purely the private expression of that teacher or staff member and do not reflect the policy of or the endorsement from the high school." It may be legal for teachers to wear such T-shirts in class, but some question whether it is appropriate for authority figures. Cliff McInturff, president of the Orange County Classroom Teachers Association, said he thought wearing such a shirt represents "an inappropriate intrusion of religious belief in the classroom. The teacher is modeling a religious

belief in a very overt way. It's too close to a subtle form of instruction."
In September of 2005, the principal of Boca Raton High School credited the rise in his school's state rating from a C to an A to prayers of
Christian groups around the country. The previous year the principal,
Geoff McKee, had been criticized for referring to God in meetings
with teachers. I reported many of these public school evangelism stories as fairly and dispassionately as I could, and I think I was successful. Yet I could not help thinking that those in the Christian
majority—if they had stopped to think about it—might not have been
so arrogant and insensitive if they had any experience as a religious
minority. Perhaps if they had spent some time in a school or society
dominated by Mormons, Muslims, or Jews who assumed that theirs
was the one true faith, they might have behaved differently.

There are many examples of complaints about secularists imping-
ing on the nation's religious heritage and character, often dealing with
Christmas and Easter displays on public property. These often include
crosses, Hanukkah menorahs, five- and six-pointed stars and Christmas trees, and the performance of holiday songs with explicitly religious lyrics. Patricia Sonntag, an administrator at California State
University at Sacramento, banned Christmas decorations at her
offices, along with celebrations of holidays like Halloween and
Valentine's Day. Joseph Loconte, a fellow at the Heritage Foundation,
was typical, writing in a column for the *San Diego Union* in 2004
about "the widespread effort to either publicly silence or sanitize the
essentially religious message of Christianity, crosses, crèches and
carols." That same year, a group called the Alliance Defense Fund created a "Christmas Project" that brought together more than seven
hundred legal activists "to combat any attempts to censor the cele-
bration of Christmas" in public spaces like town squares and public
schools. The efforts by secularists, Loconte wrote, "ignored the powerful influence of Christian belief in American civic and political
life. . . . To disdain a zeal for Christian truth . . . is to reject much of
what has made the United States a decent and democratic society."
Or, as former U.S. Senator Zell Miller put it at Justice Sunday II on
August 14, 2005, in Nashville, Tennessee, "Each Christmas [the U.S.
Supreme Court] kidnaps the baby Jesus—halo, manger, and all—from
the city square." At the same rally, Tony Perkins, president of the Family Research Council, told the crowd at Two Rivers Baptist Church

that, because of the court's public school ruling, "our children don't have a right to pray." On August 25, 2005, Franklin Graham told the Associated Press's Rachel Zoll, "There is an attempt by the secularists to take Jesus Christ and to take God out of every aspect of our society."

The controversy over the largely imaginary "War on Christmas" reached near-hysteria as the season drew near in 2005, fanned almost entirely by the cable news networks, including calls for boycotts of retail chains wishing customers "Happy Holidays." Liberty Counsel teamed with Falwell to go on the offensive. In what they dubbed "Project Grinch," the lawyer and the minister targeted groups like the ACLU and People for the American Way, who they charged wanted to take Christmas out of public schools and the public square. Staver and Falwell mobilized seven hundred attorneys and, through Falwell's e-mail newsletter, notified half a million ministers, leaders, and activists, urging them to fight for religious content in holiday celebrations, including nativity scenes and singing carols with explicitly religious lyrics. In newspaper ads, they asked their followers to designate those in public positions and retail stores as a "Friend or Foe of Christmas."

You might think that such hyperbolic whining about discrimination, as Jon Stewart suggested, is not very persuasive in the Sunbelt suburbs, where judges, like most office holders (at least the white ones) tend to be conservative, Christian, and Republican. Still, claims that religion and traditional values are embattled and subject to discrimination in schools, the workplace, and public spaces are a staple of Christian radio and television and of many pulpits. Rev. Russell Johnson of First Christian Church of Canton, Ohio, claimed that "secular jihadists" have "hijacked" this country, according to August 3, 2005, *USA Today.* A month earlier, *USA Today* reported that among the items on display at the annual convention of the CBA, formerly known as the Christian Booksellers Association, was a T-shirt featuring the tattooed image of hands folded in prayer, accompanied by the words "Legalize it." Back on April 13, 1999, when I reported on the Christian "persecution" issue for the *Orlando Sentinel,* evangelical activists were ready with a laundry list of complaints, many of which anticipated those of Indiana's outspoken Republican Congressman Hostettler. "Religious expression is under attack, and what we have been doing is standing up for the freedoms that are already constitutionally protected," said Mat Staver of Liberty Counsel. "More people are coming to us because they feel under assault." Jay Sekulow agreed. "We receive hundreds of phone calls and letters to our office each week from people who have had their rights violated," said Sekulow. "There is still tremendous hostility, or else we wouldn't be filing lawsuits all over the country." Major national institutions, especially the news media, "insistently and incessantly attack and ridicule what have been the traditional values in this culture," said Rev. Richard Land, president of the Southern Baptist Convention's Ethics and Religious Liberty Commission.

For their part, secularists and mainline denominations seem to be fighting a largely symbolic, rear-guard, and potentially self-defeating battle: like the ACLU's legal challenge of sales tax exemptions for Bibles and other sacred writings, such as the Qur'an, in Georgia and elsewhere, rather than simply appealing that other faith's books be exempted; or Americans United for the Separation of Church and State's complaints to Florida Governor Jeb Bush when he named C. S. Lewis's *The Lion, the Witch and the Wardrobe* for the state's student reading campaign. The group charged that the choice was out of sync with the Constitution because it is "filled with allusions to Christianity." The Christian right cries persecution whenever it encounters disagreement, Bill Leonard, dean of Wake Forest University Divinity School, told the Associated Press's Zoll. "They want to be culture dominant," he asserted. Certainly, leaders like Leonard see themselves as a defensive bulwark against resurgent evangelicals who are flexing their newfound political muscle. Civil-liberties groups and members of minority religions assert that evangelical Christians are trying to force their faith and ideology on an unwilling public. "The leadership of the religious right is pushing people around," said Carole Shields of Miami, president of People for the American Way, which often finds itself battling conservative Christian groups, in 1999. "They use scare tactics with their own troops in order to get grass-roots support." Marc Stern, legal director of the American Jewish Congress, said a religious gathering in south Florida where Republican congressional leaders joined "this clamor to reclaim America for Christ" was cause for concern. "There are those who sincerely believe that they have to impose their views on the culture in order to save the culture," he said.

Obviously, some of the alarmist rhetoric can be attributed to the fundraising needs of interest groups, regardless of what side of the culture war they are on. But the reality is that, depending on whether they are in Boston or Birmingham, Alabama, both sides are right. "The issue is really the nature of our pluralism," said Martin Marty of the University of Chicago's Public Religion Project. "There are two countries there—that's for certain. . . . There is still a great deal of regionalism in American religion." Academic experts and neutral observers say that politically mobilized majorities are able to flex their muscles wherever they are. In northeastern and West Coast cities and campus communities, secularists and cultural liberals set the tone. There, the news media and governmental policy tend to support and reinforce their values on issues such as racial diversity, multiculturalism, freedom of expression—especially in the arts—euthanasia, gender, and sexual orientation.

The battle over the Ten Commandments is an instructive example, both of the duplicity and opportunism of some evangelicals, and of the way some secularists can help muddy the waters. Roy Moore, former Alabama Supreme Court chief justice, placed the issue of the Ten Commandments on the national agenda in August of 2004 with his failed effort to install a two-and-a-half ton granite monument in the court's rotunda. Earlier, he gave a quantum boost to his political career by posting the Ten Commandments on the bench of his circuit courtroom after he was first elected a relatively obscure local judge. He claimed, disingenuously, that there was no religious intent to his action, but said he would not post any similar statutes or admonitions from non-Judeo-Christian traditions. Moore ran out his grandstanding effort regarding his monument when the U.S. Supreme Court refused to hear his appeal of a suit brought by the American Civil Liberties Union. His threatened defiance ultimately drove off most other evangelical leaders, who pleaded support for the "rule of law." However, many later picked up Moore's claim that the federal courts' action was part of a campaign to rip all evidence of the nation's religious heritage from public life.

In the suburbs, this sophistry was not selling. People recognized that Christian groups were part of a contemporary, organized, and—to most people—transparent effort to post religious documents in public buildings for boldly evangelical purposes, and seemed not to be troubled by lawsuits aimed at removing them. They were pushing the envelope. A week after the United States Supreme Court heard oral arguments on another Ten Commandments case, involving two Kentucky courthouses and the Texas state capitol, the Mississippi House of Representatives passed a bill permitting the public posting of a variety of religious texts and mottoes, including the Ten Commandments, "In God We Trust," and the Beatitudes from Jesus' Sermon on the Mount. "Our Founding Fathers recognized the important and necessary role religion plays in the moral foundation of our culture, and we too must ensure that this cornerstone of America's heritage is not erased from our public square," said Tim Wildmon, president of the conservative American Family Association, hailing the vote.

However, the litigation brought by some secularists to remove longer-standing monuments, erected in a more innocent time, like the Ten Commandments on the grounds of the Texas state capitol, gave some credence to the demagogues' dire warnings. That six-foot monument, one of seventeen monuments and twenty-one historical markers on twenty-two acres, was one of hundreds funded by film mogul Cecil B. DeMille to promote his 1956 film *The Ten Commandments*. Suits challenging such older, historic displays raised the specter of removing similar vestiges, like "In God We Trust" on coins and currency. Or sandblasting them from the United States Supreme Court building. The U.S. Supreme Court, which had consolidated the Kentucky and Texas cases, made the obvious (and logical) distinction between these issues in its oral arguments. Attorneys for the Kentucky courthouses argued that the fact that "the Ten Commandments influenced American law and government can hardly be questioned," making their display harmless. But Justice Antonin Scalia rejected that reasoning. "You're watering it down to say the only message is a secular message. I can't agree with you. 'Our laws come from God.' If you don't believe that sends a message, you're kidding yourself." Scalia told the lawyer defending the Texas capitol monument that the Ten Commandments are "a symbol of the fact that government derives its authority from God," and thus it is "an appropriate symbol to be on state grounds."

In two 5-4 rulings with numerous dissents, the court decided on June 27, 2005, that the Kentucky courtroom displays of the Ten Commandments would have to go. But those like the Texas monument, decades- and centuries-old, included among many symbols and sayings, including some from pre-Christian civilizations like the Babylonians and the Greeks, could stay. Justice Scalia charged that the majority in the Kentucky ruling, in effect, utilized the decision to "ratchet up the court's hostility to religion." Local, state, and national leaders of the religious right huffed and puffed and harrumphed about the court's ruling. "The court has failed to decide whether it will stand up for religious freedom of expression, or if it will allow liberal special interests to banish God from the public square," James Dobson of Focus on the Family told the *New York Times*. Dobson and others organized "Justice Sunday II" for August 14, 2005, to gather opposition to the ruling, which Tony Perkins, president of the Family Research Council, said was an example of "the court's hostility toward religion and Christianity in particular," according to the July, 15, 2005, *New York Times*. But statements like these generated no outrage in the suburbs, perhaps because the court's carefully balanced decision had struck a resonant note.

So, was America, as some evangelicals insist, a "Christian nation" from its inception? Much of this particular debate is clearly pointless, with advocates using the excerpted writings—often out of context—of various Founding Fathers to support this position, as they might trade Bible verses back and forth as theological proof texts. In the Sunbelt especially, they like to cite documents like Federalist Paper No. 2, in which John Jay wrote about "the privilege and interest of our Christian nation." Naturally, these advocates of closer ties between government and Christian faith brush aside Thomas Jefferson's letter to Danbury, Connecticut, Baptists, calling for a wall of separation between church and state, as evidence of any "original intent." Likewise Jefferson's dismissal of the book of Revelation as the ravings of a lunatic and, in a letter to John Adams, the belief that one day Jesus' virgin birth would be "classed with the fable of the generation of Minerva in the brain of Jupiter." Or James Madison's Remonstrances to the Virginia legislature on June 20, 1785, opposing all government support of religion, which he wrote to oppose "A Bill Establishing a Provision for Teachers of the Christian Religion," explicitly rejecting the notion of making Virginia a Christian state. And certainly Benjamin Franklin's view that, "When a religion is good, I conceive it will support itself; and when it does not support itself, and God does not take care to support it so that its professors are obliged to call for help of the civil power, 'tis a sign, I apprehend, of its being a bad one."

Richard Parker, a professor of religion and politics at the John F. Kennedy School of Government at Harvard University, agreed that there is a geographic disconnect over church and state, rooted in history as much as it is in culture and values. America's Founding Fathers—some of whom, the deists, held what were at the time unconventional religious beliefs—did not want their new country to establish a national church, like the Church of England. From the beginning, Parker said, "there was denominational competition that produced a lively marketplace" in which different churches vied for followers. Engraved on the wall of the Thomas Jefferson Memorial in Washington are these words, from A Bill Establishing Religious Freedom, passed by the Virginia Assembly in 1786: "No man should be compelled to frequent or support any religious worship or ministry or shall otherwise suffer on account of his religious opinions or belief." The legacy of this tradition is evident today. "America is more Christian than India is Hindu," Parker said. "But it is the case that no single Christian denomination makes up more than a quarter of the population." Parker said there is also the "frontier hypothesis" that explains regional differences. "Beginning in the early 1800s as America expanded westward, Baptist and Methodist faiths took off first in the South and then the Midwest. The Southern Baptist and Methodist churches became the de facto established churches of the South and Midwest." As a result, he said, "the Southern churches became the core repository of Southern values in the aftermath of the Civil War."

Still heavily Baptist, Methodist, and to a lesser degree Presbyterian, the South took the stance that northern Protestant churches—which had opposed slavery and then supported the Reconstruction that followed—were essentially antireligious, according to Parker. Later, in the Progressive era, the social activism of these denominations came to embody "Northern Yankee liberalism" that southern Baptists and Methodists wanted no part of. "The dominant mainline churches of the Northeast and Midwest embraced a de-emphasis on the public role of religion, and turned to the uses of government as an instrument to accomplish their social goals," he said, a trend that was generally resisted in the South after the Civil War. For conservative white southerners who controlled the power structure, political discourse was confined to the Democratic Party for nearly a century, from 1876 to 1966. The moral and cultural discourse during this period was largely restricted to conservative branches of the Baptist and Methodist churches. "It is not just that the South is the most homogeneously Protestant, and evangelical Protestant," said Parker. "It is that the pluralist reality of religion is nowhere nearly as significant there as it is in areas like the Northeast."

Many observers attribute the prevalence of conservative social values and the success of conservative candidates in the South to the belief that southerners are more religious than people in other parts of the country. Gallup Poll data support this view. At the request of the *Orlando Sentinel,* Gallup combined its results from its annual survey about religious practices from the years 1992 to 1998. More than 19,000 adults were surveyed, with a margin of error of less than 1 percent. The survey found that in the eastern region of the country, which includes New England and the Middle Atlantic states, 52 percent of adults said they found religion "very important in their lives," compared with 70 percent who felt that way in the South. Whit Ayres, an Atlanta-based pollster who works for Republican candidates, said that "as a general rule, religious orientation and especially Christian orientation is widely considered to be a plus in American politics compared to politics in other developed nations," where surveys consistently show people to be less religious in their behavior and beliefs. "So much of the regional differences are cultural," he said. "The South is the stronghold of the Baptist church that tends to be more overt in religious expression. The Northeast has been the province of Roman Catholics and upper-class Protestants for whom the quiet exercise of religion is more a priority."

Thus the geographic terrain can determine the outcome of culture war skirmishes. Religious conservatives "are still on the march in the South" and "still fighting offensive battles on the school board front," according to Rev. Barry Lynn of Americans United for the Separation of Church and State, which often finds itself allied against conservative Christian groups. But in the Northeast, it's a different story. "In Connecticut, people just don't buy the idea that Satan is taking over the schools," Lynn said. In the 1970s, northerners—the neighbors of my youth—began migrating in large numbers from the Rust Belt to the Sunbelt suburbs. Although Christians for the most part, they brought with them secularist notions about the public expression of religion. This put them into increasing conflict with their Baptist and evangelical neighbors, whose views on religion and culture had been unquestioned for decades. The result has been a series of court suits by these newer residents, like Lisa Herdahl in Mississippi, said the American Jewish Congress's Stern. Often they are the ones bringing suit against Christian prayer in the classroom—over the intercom and at graduation and football games—as well as the posting of the Ten Commandments in courtrooms and other public buildings. In response, Deep South state legislatures have proposed measures that would permit these expressions of faith, in clear violation of the Constitution. Yet for similar reasons, evangelical Christians feel beleaguered in areas of the country where they are weak, and may have to resort to litigation in self-defense, according to the Southern Baptist Convention's Richard Land. "What were the counter-culture values of the 1960s are now the ascendant values in the national culture, as best exemplified by the Northeast and the West Coast," he said.

There are some signs of hope that this pattern can be broken. On September 22, 2005, the Bible Literacy Project and the First Amendment Center copublished a Bible study guide for use in public schools. The textbook, *The Bible and Its Influence,* was written to teach the influence of the Bible on art, music, literature, and societies in general throughout the ages. About three hundred school districts are considering courses based on the guide. Some conservative Christian conservatives objected, decrying the curriculum as watered down. But groups endorsing the book included the National Association of Evangelicals and its president Ted Haggard; the American Jewish Congress; the National School Boards Association; the National Education Association; and the American Federation of Teachers. "This book is proof that the despair is premature," the American Jewish Congress's Marc Stern told Richard Ostling of the Associated Press, "that it is possible to acknowledge and respect deep religious differences and yet find some common ground." And this is not the only area of mutual agreement. Some of the concerns of the culture war also cross both geographic and ideological boundaries, according to syndicated columnist Cal Thomas. "There is a general sense that liberals and conservatives have that something is morally and culturally wrong," Thomas said. "There is a deepening cynicism in the land that certain things are beyond repair." The American Jewish Congress's Stern did not disagree: "Conservative Christians feel put upon, and need to feel put upon, by elites," he said. "And elites feel threatened by conservative Christians [who] they think are out to impose their religious values on them—and each is correct." Put another way, people with political power tend to use it to enforce their views on a variety of issues, including faith, either in the cause of religiosity (in red states) or secularism (in blue states). Those in the minority tend to resent it when they do, which is why they resort to the courts and the Constitution and media for relief. It's not exactly Lord Acton, but it's close: power corrupts; absolute power corrupts absolutely.

Despite the hopes of many evangelicals, the election of 2004 did not result in a clear-cut victory in the culture war. In fact, their victory led to some surprising divisions within evangelical ranks.

Chapter 5

Controversies and Contradictions

*N*ationally, it did not take long for evangelicals to demonstrate their internal diversity. Just months after the 2004 election, the University of Akron's John Green's polling analysis supported my own observations about the complexity of the evangelical community, specifically over the issue of environmentalism. As frequently happens, a single story in the *New York Times* put the issue on the national agenda. The March 10, 2005, piece by Laurie Goodstein, followed by another the following day for those not paying close enough attention, presented the issue to the country—and America's media. Rev. Richard Cizik, chief lobbyist for the National Association of Evangelicals (NAE), was at the head of a group of influential religious leaders who argued that "global warming is an urgent threat, a cause of poverty and Christian issue because the Bible mandates stewardship of God's creation." As Cizik told Goodstein, "I don't think God is going to ask us how he created the earth, but he will ask us what we did with what he created."

The *New York Times* article coincided with two Capitol Hill meetings called by legislative backers of a bill to limit greenhouse gasses, an issue considered anathema to Republicans and their big business supporters. Rev. Ted Haggard, president of the NAE, an umbrella organization of more than fifty church denominations and groups representing thirty million people, later joined Cizik's initiative. Haggard, who presides over a Colorado Springs megachurch, has strong conservative bona fides. As one of the nation's most influential evangelicals, he believes the United States should be governed by laws, and "not by judges" who overrule the will of the people and their elected representatives. Yet he defies predictable political pigeon-holes, even in this instance, supporting the U.S. Supreme Court's decision in the Lawrence vs. Texas case, which struck down anti-sodomy laws. "Evangelical does not mean any specific political ideology," Haggard told reporter Paul Nussbaum, in a profile for the June 19, 2005, *Philadelphia Inquirer.* "Some members of the religious right believe it is impossible to be a Bible-believing liberal. I believe you can be a Bible-believer and a liberal. People come from all ends of the spectrum."

Cizik and Haggard came to their environmentalism—a label they studiously eschewed—by different roads. Cizik told the *Times* he had been "dragged" to a conference on climate change in Oxford, England, in 2002, by Rev. Jim Ball, of the Evangelical Environmental Network. (Ball generated a media flurry in 2002 with a series of diatribes against SUVs, buying ads with the headline "What Would Jesus Drive?") Cizik called the experience a "conversion" and compared it to an "altar call," that part of the Christian service when the unsaved are invited to accept Jesus. Haggard became converted in a typically middle-class, suburban way, as some of his critics have pointed out. While scuba diving, he noticed that global warming and the resulting rise in ocean temperature, along with pollution, were damaging coral reefs.

Cizik and Ball participated in another conference on the environment in June of 2002 in Maryland, with about twenty-five other evangelical leaders, according to the *New York Times.* A seasoned lobbyist and consensus builder, Cizik knew that how an issue is framed for evangelicals would be critical to whether they would support it. The agreement in Maryland was called a "covenant," rather than a "position paper," and, in a particularly brilliant semantic stroke, they dubbed their version of environmentalism "creation care." The strategy worked. In October of 2004, Cizik, Haggard, and their association met in Atlanta to draw up a position paper entitled "For the Health of the Nation: An Evangelical Call to Civic Responsibility," ultimately signed by more than one hundred evangelical leaders. A coauthor of the document was liberal Ron Sider, founder of the left-of-center Evangelicals for Social Action. "God measures societies by how they treat people at the bottom," the paper declared. Thus, evangelicals' moral mandate should be: "To protect the vulnerable and the poor, to guard the sanctity of human life, to further racial reconciliation and justice, to renew the family, to care for creation, and to promote justice, freedom and peace." The Bible, as evangelicals read it, "implies the principle of sustainability: our uses of the earth must be designed to conserve and renew the earth rather than to deplete or destroy it." The document calls on the government "to encourage fuel efficiency, reduce pollution, encourage sustainable use of natural resources, and provide for the proper care of wildlife and their natural habitats." But despite the fact that the platform was drafted in the midst of the heated presidential campaign, it was virtually ignored by the secular media—which includes me.

In March of 2005, when the *Times* helped the issue resurface, Haggard and Cizik were separately doing some delicate maneuvering. They were fine-tuning their approach for their allies in the White House and among Congressional Republicans, while at the same time massaging the issue for their evangelical constituents. So Haggard, a free-market zealot who speaks with the White House every Monday, told Goodstein that, when it comes to limiting greenhouse gas emissions, "We want to be pro-business environmentalists." In the next two paragraphs, Cizik seemed to be justifying some regulatory limitations, but on moral grounds. "We're not averse to government-mandated prohibitions on behavioral sin such as abortions," he said. "We try to restrict it. So why, if we're social tinkering to protect the sanctity of human life, ought we not be for a little tinkering to protect the environment?" Haggard did not shrink from the significance of the event. "I think the power base is shifting" on issues beyond the environment, he told the *Philadelphia Inquirer,* away from the same old faces and talking heads like Robertson and Falwell. "We think differently from the previous generation, the 1980s Moral Majority crowd." Later Haggard told the *Washington Post,* "The environment is a values issue. There are significant and compelling theological reasons why it should be a banner issue for the Christian right."

Liberal media commentators, some still not recovered from the November presidential election results and the political ascendancy of the evangelicals, rushed to celebrate, albeit with some caution. "This could give a whole new meaning to the phrase culture war," Jane Eisner wrote in a column for the *Philadelphia Inquirer* of March 18, 2005. "Let's be honest: environmentalists could learn a thing or

two from evangelicals about promoting values and vision." Edward
Helmore, writing in the *Guardian* of London, on April 20, 2005, spec-
ulated that the move by evangelicals on the environment "could mark
the beginning of a significant shift in the character and temperament
of the U.S."

These, and more effusive commentaries hailing a possible coalition
of Democratic greens and Republican evangelicals, in turn provoked
a conservative evangelical backlash among "leaders," commentators,
and activists who saw their hegemony—if not their monopoly—and
influence threatened. The National Association of Evangelicals is no
liberal evangelical splinter group or think tank; it is broad-based and
centrist in the evangelical context (Later, it would ask to join the Air
Force legal defense against charges of allowing inappropriate proselytizing at the service academy in Colorado Springs.), which is why
its actions were seen as such a threat to those accustomed to speaking
for evangelicals. Syndicated columnist and author Cal Thomas wrote
that Cizik and Haggard's effort was "doomed because it distracts and
dilutes the primary calling of evangelicals . . . The social gospel is
about causes, not Christ. . . . It's a subtle but effective means of dis-
tracting evangelicals from their paramount calling, which is about conversion, not politics." Thomas, coauthor of *Blinded by Might,* which
argued that the religious right has overplayed its political hand and
politicized its gospel, predicted that this would be "another failed
effort that will lead many astray, divert resources from more effective
pursuits and leave little of eternal value." Tom Minnery, vice president
of Focus on the Family, urged evangelicals to avoid debating global
warming. "The issues of marriage, the issues of pro-life are the issues
that define us to this day," he told a luncheon gathering, according to
the March 11, 2005, *New York Times.* "The issue of global warming
does not characterize evangelicalism," he told Religion News Service.
An official statement from Focus said, "Any issue that seems to put
plants and animals above humans is one we cannot support." Some of
the more theologically extreme evangelicals—called "dispensational-
ists"—argued that there is no need to focus on stewardship of the earth
and the environment, because the end of the world is near.

However, in the face of assertions that evangelicals hold the same,
predictable positions on a spectrum of issues—war, gun control, public school prayer, capital punishment, and government interventions

in cases like Terri Schiavo, as well as the impending apocalypse—more liberal evangelicals like Martin Marty, emeritus professor of religion at the University of Chicago, demurred. "These are the only things most mass communicators communicate about when they deal with that one-fourth of America whose religious preferences get them named 'evangelicals,'" he wrote in his online column "Sightings," on June 20, 2005, produced by the University of Chicago Divinity School. "Many evangelicals complain that this is unfair—and rightfully so, since they don't want to be, and shouldn't be, clumped together with the readily noted strident and aggressive sorts. . . . They are less fascinating, less alluring, less easy to identify and cover than are the media-favored aggressives, but they are making a point and making a dent." The devoutly nonpolitical evangelist Luis Palau made a similar point, telling hundreds of pastors at First Presbyterian Church of Orlando on October 19, 2005, that, by allowing others to speak for evangelicals, "we've given the image that we're nuts!" Even at conservative intellectual centers, like Fuller Theological Seminary in Pasadena, California, there are those who object to this assumption that all evangelicals are right-wing. "Many of us who consider ourselves to be evangelical Christians would want to distance ourselves from that kind of alignment," Edmund Gibbs, a Fuller professor, told the *Philadelphia Inquirer.* The conservative evangelical author Os Guinness agreed. The influential cultural critic told the *New York Times'* Goodstein, on January 8, 2006, "I know hundreds of people who are just terminally frustrated with the idiotic public statements of Jerry Falwell and Pat Robertson and the idea that these people represent us. They don't."

There is evidence that evangelical support for some form of environmentalism is not confined to the upper reaches of organizations like the National Association of Evangelicals. *Newsweek,* in its August 18, 2005, cover report on spirituality, devoted one story in the package to what it called "Green Religion," or "Eco-Christianity." The focus was on Allen Johnson, of Dunsmore, West Virginia, a minister who founded a twenty-member group called Christians for the Mountains to defend the local environment from the ravages of powerful coal operators and their influential lobbyists. "God has called all of us seriously," Johnson told the magazine, "and we should agree on one thing: we should take care of his earth." A member of the conservative Pentecostal Word of Faith Church, Johnson was inspired to activism by a missionary trip to Haiti in 1993. The message he brings to fellow evangelicals, sometimes via PowerPoint presentations, is simple and biblical: "The earth is the Lord's, and everything in it." Johnson emphasized to *Newsweek* that, like Cizik and Haggard, his personal agenda is religious, rather than political. "My identity is not as an environmentalist," he said. "It's as a Christian. Because I am a Christian I should be involved with social justice, the poor, the needy. Environmentalism is one thing in my circle, but it's not my center." The dilemma for the Democrats was summed up by Joel Gillespie, a conservative Christian, writing in the Spring 2005 issue of *On Earth* magazine. "I'll admit that when I pushed the button for President Bush, I did so with some sadness, given his dismal environmental record," he wrote.

> But many of us who love the natural world feel we face an almost impossible either-or predicament. Voting for pro-environment candidates usually means voting for a package of other policies that we will never swallow. We're forced to choose unborn babies or endangered species, traditional marriage or habitat protection, cleaning the smut that comes across the airwaves or the smut that fouls our air. And the fact that we are forced to make such choices has harmed the natural environment and the special places we love and cherish.

Ultimately, in the face of determined Bush administration opposition, the bipartisan environmental effort to limit greenhouse gases failed in the U.S. Senate. Months later, on a warm, late September night in Miami Beach, Cizik told me about the behind-the-scenes maneuvering that took place in Washington during the battle—and after. Over plates of Cuban food, served outside on the Lincoln Road mall, he regaled me and two other journalists attending the annual convention of the Religion Newswriters Association with tales of how his opponents did their best to marginalize him and other progressive evangelicals. Meetings were held on Capitol Hill with leaders of more conservative evangelical organizations, aimed at undermining Cizik. This led to a "Letter to the National Association of Evangelicals," signed by Charles Colson, James Dobson, Richard Land, and Donald Wildmon, of the American Family Association, asking that the NAE staff (e.g., Cizik) not speak to climate change issues. With eighteen others, they wrote that global warming "is not a consensus issue . . . We are evangelicals, and we care about God's creation. However, we believe there should be room for Bible-believing evangelicals to disagree about the cause, severity and solutions to the global warming issue." NAE leaders acceded to the request, but that muzzling was not enough for some. Oil-state congresspersons and White House operatives attempted to paint this self-described "Bush Republican" as a dangerous radical, Cizik said, to the point that Oklahoma Senator James Inhofe tried to get him fired as the NAE's lobbyist. Inhofe, chair of the Senate Environment and Public Works Committee, does not believe that global warming is the result of human-made gases. In an interview with Pat Robertson, he claimed that the NAE was locked in an embrace with "far-Left environmentalists." Robertson agreed, suggesting that Haggard was "a little naive." The next morning in Miami, Cizik returned to the theme, telling the assembled religion reporters from around the country to think more expansively about evangelicals. "We are not the stereotypes we are portrayed as," he said. "We believe in pluralism."

Despite the defeat over limiting gas emission, hope is still resilient. In September of 2005, a group called the Academy of Evangelical Scientists and Ethicists joined with the Coalition on the Environment and Jewish Life in an effort dubbed the Noah Alliance. The group cited biblical authority in its joint effort to oppose Republican plans to weaken and roll back the Endangered Species Act. Cizik, appearing on public radio's *Living on Earth* show on October 22, 2005, acknowledged that evangelicals might not be able to make the environment a major issue in the 2008 presidential election. At the same time, he said, politicians listen to NAE members, especially in states where they are traditionally strong. And if evangelicals put their "imprimatur" on this issue, candidates will notice.

On February 8, 2006, the curtain rose on the second act of the great eco-evangelism drama, beginning much like the first act, with a *New York Times* article by Laurie Goodstein. The piece outlined what would happen later that morning at the National Press Club in Washington: the unveiling of another environmental effort called "The Evangelical Climate Initiative," aimed at heading off global warming. The document was signed by eighty-six leaders, including Todd Bassett, national commander of the Salvation Army; Rich Stearns, president of World Vision; Duane Litfin, president of Wheaton College; Jo Anne Lyon, executive director of World Hope International; and Jim Ball, of the Evangelical Environmental Network. Megachurch pastors included Rick Warren of Saddleback; Rev. Jack Hayford, of Foursquare Gospel Church; Leith Anderson, of Wooddale Church, outside Minneapolis, and a former NAE president; and Joel Hunter, of Central Florida's Northland Church.

In taking the political temperature of the Sunbelt suburbs, Hunter's invitation to be a spokesperson—and his acceptance—was probably more significant than that of the more recognizable names. Northland's average weekend service attendance in Longwood, Florida, is 8,000, most of whom are white and politically conservative. En route to Washington, he told me that he felt he had been asked to participate because "They needed a pastor from a state that was going to face some significant environmental issues in the future," and that Florida, with its exploding population and declining water table, and concerns with offshore drilling, and preserving the Everglades and other wetlands, qualified. When he agreed, organizers asked that he appear in a national, thirty-second TV spot for Fox News Network and CNN, as well as in about a dozen regional markets around the country, including Florida. At first, he had turned it down, but then he accepted. "Why is this important? It's not so much an ideological or political issue as it is a moral and biblical issue." In the commercial, Hunter asks, "Do you know that evangelical leaders are telling us that global warming will produce even more devastating floods and disasters and disease on the earth? As Christians, our faith in Jesus Christ compels us to love our neighbors and to be stewards of God's creation. The good news is that with God's help, we can stop global warming, for our kids, for our world, and for our Lord."

Noticeably absent from the declaration, which appeared as a full-page ad in the February 9 *New York Times*, were the names of Richard Cizik and Ted Haggard. Cizik told me a week earlier that they did not join "in order to respect the reality within the movement, namely that not all evangelicals were ready to accept climate change as a priority on the evangelical agenda." Nonetheless, their fingerprints were all over the stage-managed production. Cizik, whose family by now owned two hybrid cars, told Goodstein he had helped recruit signers and sponsors, and he later gave an extensive interview supporting the effort to BBC radio. Haggard offered the *Times* a personal endorsement for Goodstein's story: "There is no doubt about it in my mind that climate change is happening, and there is no doubt that it would be wise for us to stop doing the foolish things we're doing that could potentially be causing this. In my mind there is no downside to being cautious." The *Times'* exclusive—other journalists, including myself, were constrained by an embargo—served its purpose, alerting the media and guaranteeing greater coverage, including British coverage that played the initiative as a direct, unprecedented challenge to Bush administration policies. The crux of the initiative was endorsement of "cost-effective, market-based mechanisms" to limit carbon dioxide emissions, the same approach offered in a 2005 Senate resolution by Republican Pete Domenici and Democrat Jeff Bingaman, both of New Mexico.

Apart from moral suasion and biblical justification, sponsors of the initiative offered the results of a poll of 1,000 born-again and evangelical Protestants in September 2005, conducted by Ellison Research. The survey found that 63 percent said global warming is a problem that should be addressed today; assuming global warming is occurring, and is caused by human action, 51 percent said that steps should be taken, even if there is a high cost to the United States; and 70 percent felt that global warming will pose a serious threat to future generations. I was curious about what was beneath those results, so later in the day I called Ron Sellers, president of Ellison, and asked him to run the same questions just for white evangelicals, who comprised 73 percent of the survey. There was still support, although not as dramatic: 58 percent felt global warming should be addressed today; 50 percent agreed that efforts should be made, even at significant cost; and 65 percent said global warming will pose a serious threat to future generations. The number of whites answering that Christians should generally support environmental issues, 55 percent, was even greater than the overall response of 54 percent.

At the press conference, Jim Ball called the list of signers and sponsors "centrist." World Hope International's Lyon, aiming for the evangelical (and semantic) high ground, put the issue in perspective. Since the 1980s, she said, some evangelicals have seen the environment "as a pro-life issue." The document was in no sense

radical, lauding major multinational corporations—and periodic pol-
luters—like General Electric, BP, DuPont, Duke Energy, and Shell
for their cooperation and support. The evangelicals also acknowledged financial support for the efforts by major philanthropic organizations, like Rockefeller Brothers Foundation, the Pew Charitable
Trusts, and the Hewlett Foundation. Within hours, the Environmental Defense president Fred Krupp picked up the centrist theme. "This
statement marks nothing less than a historic tipping point," he said,
spinning furiously. "Global warming isn't a liberal issue or an issue
that concerns just conservationists. Taking action—now—is a matter
of values. It's a moral issue, a mainstream issue that reflects a national
consensus. These courageous leaders have said that global warming
should be a concern to all who value God's creation and that's a mainstream, nonpartisan message that makes sense whether you're in
South Carolina, Arkansas, California, or Minnesota. Their support for
a pro-business solution makes all the sense in the world. Capping
greenhouse gas emissions will unleash a wave of American innovation. It will create new jobs, and it'll give the economy a boost."

But conservative evangelicals were having none of it. In a dueling
press release, a group called the Interfaith Stewardship Alliance,
organized by Dr. E. Calvin Beisner, associate professor of historical
theology at Knox Theological Seminary in Ft. Lauderdale, listed
some of the evangelical heavyweights who had not signed the global
warming document. They included: James Dobson of Focus on the
Family; Rev. D. James Kennedy of Coral Ridge Presbyterian Church;
Rev. John Hagee of Cornerstone Church; Lou Sheldon, of the Traditional Values Coalition; and Donald Wildmon of the American Family
Association. Beisner also pointed out the absence of NAE participation
in the statement—although twenty-two of the organization's board
members were among the eighty-six signers. Claiming that "the science is not settled on global warming," Beisner said, "While there is
lots of debate about the causes and hazards of climate change and how
best to respond to it, there is no debate about the Bible's priority on
helping the world's poor to improve their lot. By declining to embrace
anti-warming policies that would delay economic development and
access to clean air, clean water, and reliable food and energy supplies
in poor countries, we and the NAE together are putting the needs of
the poor at the forefront." Senator Imhofe's Capitol Hill office issued

a news release reminding Senate colleagues that the NAE had earlier reversed course on its stand on global warming. Rev. Richard Land, of the Southern Baptist Convention's Ethics and Religious Liberty Commission, told me he had not been asked to sign, but that he would have refused. Although the listing of affiliated churches, denominations, and organizations was for identification only, Land said that, practically, was a distinction without a difference. "Now you have a coalition of evangelicals who are convinced and who believe that among the constituencies they represent that there is a consensus on the causes and some of the remedies for global warming," he said. "Among Southern Baptists, there is no consensus on this issue, and absolutely no consensus on the remedies." While he wouldn't have signed the document, Land said, "I agree with much of it personally—with the caveats that you have to take into account economic and business concerns. I've been talking about this issue for years. I agree with much of what is stated in the document personally. In my books, I've been trying to foster debate and build consensus. God's going to hold us to accountable for our stewardship of his earth, but that is different from worshiping the earth."

The environmental dialogue has set the stage for a much larger debate, which survives, about whether evangelicals could make common cause on a spectrum of other issues with groups on the left with whom they have fundamental differences. A front-page story in the June 15, 2005, issue of *USA Today* was headlined "Christian right's alliances bend political spectrum." Reporter Susan Page wrote that evangelicals "have forged coalitions with—or sometimes simply pulled in the same direction as—activists who more often are their adversaries." These issues ranged from domestic, supporting measures to reduce prison rape and establishing a "living wage," to the international, fighting sex traffic, forgiving Third World debt, working against genocide and slavery in Sudan, as well as against religious persecution around the globe. A Republican congressman told a meeting of the Statesmanship Institute, a Capitol Hill program for aspiring evangelical politicians, sponsored by televangelist D. James Kennedy, that God inspired the lawmaker to oppose President Bush on the Iraq war by calling for a timetable for withdrawal, according to the *Los Angeles Times.* In August of 2005, Cizik spoke out against Pat Robertson's televised call to assassinate Venezuelan President

Hugo Chavez, telling the *Times'* Goodstein that the comments were "unfortunate and particularly irresponsible," and not representative of "most evangelical leaders." At our dinner in Miami, Cizik mocked other evangelical leaders for their failure to criticize Robertson in this instance and for their defense, more recently, of former House majority leader Tom DeLay, following his indictments. Haggard was equally outspoken regarding the Chavez remarks: "Pat doesn't speak for evangelicals any more than Dr. Phil speaks for mental health professionals." Even the Southern Baptists' Richard Land joined other evangelical leaders in condemning Robertson in early 2006 for proclaiming that Ariel Sharon's stroke was divine punishment for dividing the Land of Israel by returning Gaza to the Palestinians. The televangelist seemed in danger of becoming his movement's crazy aunt in the attic, despite his subsequent apology to the Sharon family. In early March 2006, the National Religious Broadcasters, which named Robertson Broadcaster of the Year in 1989, rejected him for a seat on the organization's board of directors, which he had held for thirty years. NRB president Frank Wright told the *Washington Post* that "there was broad dismay with some of Pat's comments and a feeling they were not helpful to Christian broadcasters in general."

"Evangelicals have broadened their perspective and widened their agenda," the University of Akron's Green told the *New York Times*. "It's not as if the social issues have vanished; they still care about them. But foreign policy issues, environmental issues, even social welfare issues have joined the agenda. That has led them to develop broader alliances in some really odd ways," said the coauthor of *The Values Campaign: The Christian Right in American Politics.* Or, as Duke University Divinity School's David C. Steinmetz observed in an October 8, 2005, Op-Ed column in the *Orlando Sentinel,* "theological orthodoxy is not at odds with social reform, but demands it." Larry Eskridge of the Institute for the Study of American Evangelicals at Wheaton College, in Wheaton, Illinois, agreed. This marriage of convenience, if that is what it is, "offers the possibility on both sides to derail the demonization process," he told the *Times*. "It maybe offers the possibility of at least getting both sides to hear and respect the other's point of view—initiating dialogue and maybe thinking your opposite doesn't have horns growing out of their head." David Brooks, the neoconservative (but not always predictable) Op-Ed columnist for the *New York Times,* listened to a talk in Washington by *The Purpose Driven Life*'s Rick Warren and came to an even more profound conclusion. "We can have a culture war in this country, or we can have a war on poverty, but we can't have both," he wrote in his May 26, 2005, column. "The natural alliance for antipoverty measures at home and abroad is between liberals and evangelical Christians. These are the only two groups that are really hyped up about these problems and willing to devote time and money to ameliorating them. If liberals and evangelicals don't get together on antipoverty measures, then there will be no majority for them and they won't get done."

Still, few if any of these social and economic issues have caught fire so far at the suburban grass roots in my part of the Sunbelt. However, another controversy ignited some fireworks within the evangelical movement, closer to ground level, several months after the dispute over environmental policy, also in May of 2005. The evangelical movement in America has no uncontested theological capital—no Vatican, no Jerusalem. As I have suggested above, there are some near candidates, including Colorado Springs in the West and Orlando in the Southeast. Other contenders include Wheaton College, in Illinois, which Billy Graham and many other evangelical leaders attended, and Calvin College in Grand Rapids, Michigan. I was invited to speak at a literary festival at Calvin in April of 2004, and during the days I spent there I found the faculty and students lively and open-minded. This may have something to do with the college's location—in a midwestern, usually Democratic state and a congressional district that regularly sent moderate Republican Gerald Ford to Washington, rather than in a Sunbelt GOP bastion. Or it may have something to do with Calvin's denominational roots. The school is affiliated with the Christian Reformed Church, which is descended from the Dutch Reformed Church, with a history of progressive stances on social and economic issues, as well as its conservative theology.

So I was not at all surprised when, following a White House announcement that George Bush would be Calvin's commencement speaker on May 21, 2005, opposition erupted on campus, where some were concerned that the invitation would be interpreted as a blanket approval of some of Bush's more controversial policies. "The real concern was what it might signal to the rest of the country," said Quentin Schultze, who holds the Arthur H. DeKruyter Chair in Faith and Communications. Calvin is no stranger to politics or controversy; one of the 2000 presidential debates took place at the school, and a 2001 speech by the late Chief Justice William Rehnquist provoked some grumbling. But this time, the issue was of a different magnitude. Calvin would be one of only two commencement addresses Bush would deliver this spring, the other being at the U.S. Naval Academy. And after four and a half years of the Bush presidency, the administration's policies were beginning to chafe some on the Calvin faculty and staff, as well as among the student body of four thousand. Three weeks before the president's visit, Jim Wallis, a left-wing evangelical and author of *God's Politics: Why the Right Gets It Wrong and the Left Doesn't Get It,* spoke on campus, packing the 770-seat chapel. He advised students not to oppose the Bush invitation, but to use the opportunity and its media limelight to offer more progressive policy alternatives.

Opposition to the commencement address first took the form of two paid advertisements in the local paper, the *Grand Rapids Press.* The Friday before the president's speech, a full-page ad appeared, paid for (at a cost of $9,500) by close to eight hundred alumni, some students, and many others who identified themselves as "friends." It was in the form of an open letter to Bush and read:

> In our view, the policies and actions of your administration, both domestically and internationally over the past four years, violate many deeply held principles of Calvin College. . . . Your deeds, Mr. President—neglecting the needy to coddle the rich, desecrating the environment and misleading the country into war—do not exemplify the faith we live by. . . . Many of your supporters are using religion as a weapon to divide our nation and advance a narrow partisan agenda.

They called on Bush to "repudiate the false claims of supporters who say that those who oppose your policies are the enemies of religion." The next day, nearly 150 current and retired faculty and staff took out a half-page ad (for $2,600) that featured an open, more mildly worded letter to Bush. "As Christians," it read, "we are called to be peacemakers and to initiate war only as a last resort. We believe your

administration has launched an unjust and unjustified war in Iraq."
The letter also cited "conflicts between our understanding of what
Christians are called to do and many of the policies of your administration." David Crump, a professor of religion who helped draft the
letter, told *Detroit News* columnist Laura Berman that the Calvin
opposition had tapped into "a silent majority in the Christian evangelical community that resents the Christian vocabulary being
hijacked by the religious right. . . . The largest part of our concern is
the way in which our religious discourse in this country has largely
been co-opted by the religious right and their wholesale endorsement
of this administration."

Across the street from the campus there were about a dozen protesters, but inside, Bush got a respectful hearing, considerable
applause, and several standing ovations. Opponents among the nine
hundred graduates wore buttons, armbands, and stickers on their
gowns and mortarboards. Between 10 and 25 percent of them had buttons reading, "God is not a Democrat or a Republican." One student
pasted a sign on her mortarboard that said, "Who Would Jesus
Bomb?" Sarah Page, a graduating senior from Chicago, exemplified
some of the mixed feelings the students had. She wore a protest button on her gown, but told the *Los Angeles Times* that she supported
the Bush invitation to speak. "I don't want people to think that being
Christian means you have to be Republican." Bush cut his scheduled
remarks from forty-five minutes to fifteen minutes—the traditional
time slot for previous commencement speakers—and in his talk he
appeared to respond to the protesters. He told the graduates and their
families that they had "a great responsibility to serve and love others,
a responsibility that goes back to the greatest commandment." This,
Bush added, "isn't a Democratic idea. This isn't a Republican idea.
This is an American idea." In all, the press estimated that a third of
the faculty opposed Bush's appearance, and that, in the 2004 election,
about 20 percent voted Democratic. Press coverage of the controversy
became a sore point among Calvin's majority.

On the Calvin Web site and in the Grand Rapids paper, college
president Gaylen J. Byker presented his own analysis of the president's visit, which he declared was "overwhelmingly positive." While
there had been some disagreement about the appearance, there was
no protest, "as inaccurately reported in some media accounts." He

criticized two Calvin professors for appearing on the Fox News Channel's *Hannity and Colmes,* where one proudly proclaimed that Calvin was no Liberty University, the fundamentalist Baptist school founded by the Rev. Jerry Falwell. Byker pointed out a previous Op-Ed column in the *Grand Rapids Press* by communications professor Randall Bytwerk defending the Bush appearance, which also appeared the day of commencement but did not attract nearly the same media attention as the two protest ads. Byker noted that a majority of the Calvin community did not sign the faculty and staff ad, which he characterized as "harshly worded." This, he said, was because they "feared that the media and the media audiences would construe the statement as disrespectful protest and a challenge of the President's Christian faith."

Some faculty were equally outspoken in the days and weeks after the visit. Schultze told me, "The coverage of this issue was very poor leading up to the event," and only marginally better thereafter. "The real story is the media's superficial understanding of a place like Calvin coupled with their emphasis on conflict," said Schultze, who has been a reliable and incisive source for me for nearly twenty years. A writer for *Christianity Today* dismissed the whole matter as a tempest in a teapot, the secular media making the obvious discovery that evangelicals sometime disagree. Another Calvin faculty member, Roy Anker, said that the goal of those who spoke up was simply "to get out the idea that Calvin is not a monolithic, right-wing Christian entity."

In that sense, the uproar succeeded, said Dale Brown, of the English faculty, whom I met in Grand Rapids in 2004. But Brown seemed conflicted about the controversy. Brown said he was impressed that Calvin was on Bush's radar and applauded Byker's help in offering the invitation. And he told me he thought the media got it wrong by characterizing it as a "protest. The faculty letter was simply opportunistic—seizing the chance while the spotlight was here to register a demurral" of the implied policy and political endorsement the commencement invitation conveyed. Yet in the end Brown signed the tough faculty letter—something he admits was out of character for the self-described moderate—and decided not to attend the speech, opting instead to stay in his office to grade final exams. Why? In the old evangelistic tradition, he believed that sitting in the faculty section beneath the podium when Bush spoke "would have been to signify silently a respect I cannot conjure for this president." In light of Brown's feelings about the Iraq war, it was something he could not do: "I believe that we have been seriously misled, even deceived, by this president." In the past decade, he wrote in an unpublished essay, Calvin College has encountered conflicting "market pressures," some urging it to follow the fundamentalist, Bob Jones University model, others looking in a secular direction, with a model like Amherst College. In the end, the Bush commencement controversy demonstrated that Calvin "turns out to be a place where many voices are informing the conversation. Although I lament the divisions that the president's visit brought to the fore, I am pleased that this is just the sort of place where someone might get a real education as opposed to, say, an indoctrination."

Another reflective faculty member, philosophy professor James K. A. Smith, chose to attend a wedding rather than the commencement. Mulling over the controversy in his May 29, 2005, blog, he said that members of the community first needed to ask themselves, "Why was it that so many in Calvin's constituency—and many others in West Michigan   eagerly welcomed President Bush into a central ritual of our college community? Why is it that the Reformed [Church's] cultural elite have come to so closely identify being faithful with being committed to a party that privileges the wealthy, is aggressively militaristic, and caters to the nouveau riche of late capitalism? . . . If we find the climate of highly churched West Michigan to be so complicit with institutionalized social injustice, then we have no one to blame but ourselves. Clearly, our churches, far from forming us otherwise, are actually contributing to the formation of docile subjects of the GOP machine."

The abundant anecdotal and statistical evidence of internal diversity among evangelicals has done little to assuage some influential blue-state critics. In sharp contrast to cable TV, where they get a largely uncritical forum, evangelicals tend to take it on the chin in print and public television. Journalists like Bill Moyers, Frank Rich, and Richard Goldstein in particular have written eloquently—and scathingly—about the rise of evangelical power and influence in America. While the baggage these commentators bring to the controversy colors their criticisms, there are valid points tucked into their personal valises. Moyers, an ordained Southern Baptist minister from Texas, is still bitter about the conservative takeover of his denomination twenty-five years ago, and no less about its subsequent emergence as a major backer of the GOP, which he sees as a major threat to the nation. "Some of these Christian conservatives are implacable," Moyers said in a keynote address at the convention of the Society of Environmental Journalists, in Austin, Texas, on October 1, 2005. "They have given their proxies to the televangelists, pastors, and preachers who have signed on with the Republican Party to turn their faith into a political religion, a weapon of partisan conflict." Rich, a liberal *New York Times* columnist, rails against political and cultural hypocrisy. The same people who piously clamor for tightened "decency" limits by the Federal Communications Commission boost the ratings for guilty pleasures like ABC-TV's *Desperate Housewives.* And Goldstein, longtime writer for the *Village Voice,* now writing for *The Nation,* is legitimately angry about the homophobic crusade he sees. At least as astringent—if more nuanced—analysis has come from observers at a greater remove. Witness an exhaustive newspaper series by Ian Brown in the *Toronto Globe and Mail* and the book, *The Right Nation: Conservative Power in America,* by the British journalists John Micklethwait and Adrian Wooldridge.

A good example of this kind of snarky outsider coverage was the May 2005 issue of *Harper's* magazine, a cover package entitled "Soldiers of Christ." Two devastating pieces, one on the National Association of Evangelicals' Ted Haggard and the other on the National Religious Broadcasters, were accompanied by an essay, "The Wrath of the Lamb," by *Harper's* editor Lewis H. Lapham, in which he wrote, "we err on the side of folly if we continue to grant the boon of tolerance to people who mean to do us harm." (That sentiment is reciprocated elsewhere in the magazine in Chris Hedges's article about the National Religious Broadcasters, in which he quotes the NRB's president, Frank Wright: "Today, calls for tolerance are often a subterfuge, because they will tolerate just about anything except Christian truth.") The magazine's issue was too much for Calvin College's James K. A. Smith, a self-proclaimed fan of *Harper's.* "Not having seen middle Americans who actually believe in God, these journalists cum anthropologists are simultaneously awed, bewildered, fascinated, and frightened by what they find," he wrote in the June 30, 2005, "Sightings," the University of Chicago's online commentary. "It is just this tone that contributes to the martyr complex that comfortable, middle-class white folks feel" in the suburbs. "If, as an evangelical, I am disturbed by what I see played out under the banner of the religious right, I know that countering this won't be accomplished by witty, sardonic editorials in my favorite magazines."

To be sure, as Smith acknowledged, there are parts of the evangelical movement that are "downright spooky" and others that are part of a "creepy netherworld." I agree, and would add that there is also manifest from time to time a streak of meanness and narrow-mindedness, self-righteousness, and nineteenth-century Know-Nothingism at the grass roots of evangelical Christianity, as well as at the top of the movement. And there is ample evidence for this feeling, although fear or suspicion might be better words. Undeniably, there are some on the Christian right who, if they ever got the whip hand, would have no compunction about jamming their religion down other people's throats, those called "Dominionists," who are determined to turn this country into a "Christian nation." As Rev. D. James Kennedy, the Florida megachurch pastor and televangelist, put it, "Our job is to reclaim America for Christ, whatever the cost. We are to exercise godly dominion and influence over our neighborhoods, our schools, our government, our literature and arts, our sports arenas, our entertainment media, our news media, our scientific endeavors—in short, over every aspect and institution of human society." A 2005 study of conduct at the United States Air Force Academy, documenting inappropriate behavior by upper-class students, faculty, staff, and even chaplains toward nonevangelical Christians, is just one recent example of this tendency.

Still, I maintain that this aspect is overrepresented and thus exaggerated in the movement's public face. To a certain degree, this is inevitable, given the superheated, cable-and-controversy-driven media environment that shapes press coverage and public understanding. "Perhaps you didn't know that Christian fundamentalists were running the United States, but then perhaps you weren't attending any upscale Manhattan parties over the holiday season," wrote Peter Steinfels, in his "Beliefs" column in the *New York Times* on January 29, 2005. Not surprising, since most of the people the writer encountered "had about as much personal contact with Christian fundamentalists as with Martians."

This anxiety about the political rise of evangelicals was not simply liberal paranoia. The election of 2004 did set the stage for some serious debates about the realistic expectations of Christian conservatives—and the reactions of liberals and Democrats.

Chapter 6

What Do They Want? (And Is It Too Late to Stop Them?)

*T*he campaign and election of 2004 were unquestionably a watershed for evangelicals in the Sunbelt and their conservative Catholic allies, characterized by unprecedented wooing and success at the polls. During the campaign, GOP strategists went to extraordinary lengths to mobilize the party's conservative religious base, much as Democrats have done for years in black churches. In June of 2004, the Bush campaign requested membership lists from evangelical churches, provoking an outcry from religious leaders. Even Southern Baptist leader Richard Land criticized the effort, calling it "a very dangerous thing" that "shouldn't be done." In September, the Republican National Committee sent a mass mailing to voters in West Virginia and Arkansas, suggesting that if John Kerry won the election, Bible reading might be banned. Here again Land said this mailing was also going "a bit too far." During a Vatican visit in early 2004, the president asked officials to mobilize U.S. bishops on election issues such as abortion and same-sex marriage, according to the *National Catholic Reporter.* But the pressure was most intense among evangelicals. At the East Waynesville Baptist Church in western North Carolina, nine members said they were forced out of the congregation by their pastor, Chan Chandler, for planning to vote for Kerry.

As a result of these and other, less controversial efforts, Republican candidates were returned to the White House and maintained their majorities in both houses of Congress. Citing exit polls, Land estimated that 78 percent of evangelical Christians voted for Bush. Nearly 24 percent of voters said after the election that "moral values" were "the one issue that mattered most" to them, more than any other group that went decisively for the GOP. Candidates backed by evangelicals made gains in legislatures and governors' mansions. In states like Florida, they also controlled many county commissions and city councils. As a result of these victories, worried blue-state residents— many of whom fully expected to recapture the White House at least— asked, what, exactly, did red-state evangelicals want? Rev. Barry Lynn of Americans United for the Separation of Church and State suggested that leaders of the Religious Right would "expect to be handsomely rewarded" for their support at the polls, warning of "TV preachers calling the shots in Washington."

For their part, America's conservative religious leaders, credited with providing the margin of victory for President Bush's victory, were ready to present the White House with a bill for services rendered. The list, they said, was a lengthy one, beginning with the nomination of U.S. Supreme Court justices who would overturn the landmark Roe v. Wade decision on abortion; increased support for a constitutional amendment banning gay marriage; and a larger role in policing decency for the Federal Communications Commission. Bob Jones III, president of Bob Jones University in South Carolina, was among the least bashful. He sent a note to Bush just a day after the election, advising, "If you have weaklings around you who do not share your biblical values, shed yourself of them. . . . Put your agenda on the front burner and let it boil," he wrote. "You owe the liberals nothing." Land, a strong Bush supporter who launched his own national voter-registration and motivation drive in a seventy-seven-foot tractor-trailer, called "iVoteValues.com," voiced similar expectations. "One of my jobs is to never be satisfied," he said, predicting the proposed amendment banning gay marriage would be added to the Constitution. With White House backing, he said, it would pass the U.S. Senate by the required two-thirds majority. By that time it had already passed in the House by a simple majority, and he predicted it would be ratified by three-fourths of the nation's state legislatures.

Directly in Land's sight was the demonstrated ability of the Senate's Democratic minority to block judicial nominations by filibustering. Pat Robertson wrote in his book *Courting Disaster,* and repeated after the election, that an "out-of-control judiciary" was a threat "more serious than al Qaeda." With an increased margin, Land said, Republicans would change Senate rules, preventing the minority from using unlimited debate to block court appointments. This would open the door to new justices who could reverse Roe v. Wade. The American Center for Law and Justice's Jay Sekulow said confirming such nominees would now be more likely. However, the attorney said he was not so certain that enough justices could be appointed in four years to reverse the abortion decision. New judges could overturn other close decisions defining church-state relations, such as permitting prayer at high-school football games and graduation ceremonies, Sekulow said. They also might uphold another congressional ban on late-term abortions, which the federal court rejected earlier. National conservative religious leaders also said they wanted to further limit federal support for stem-cell research; increase "abstinence-only" sex education; and ban human cloning and international population programs that include abortion. Statewide groups of evangelicals like the Texas Restoration Project were formed to keep up the pressure on the White House and lawmakers.

At the same time, some leaders and activists were more pragmatic about what they could expect from the second Bush administration and the GOP-controlled Congress. They acknowledged that gains might come with policy decisions and executive orders, which do not require congressional approval. One area dear to conservative Christians involves television and radio. Some advocated that the Federal Communications Commission impose even tighter decency standards on broadcast media, well beyond those instituted after incidents involving Janet Jackson's Super Bowl appearance and radio shock jock Howard Stern. Others raised the possibility of bringing some cable television and radio—where sex, nudity, violence, and profane language are common—under the FCC, to which broadcasters have been subject. "We strongly support both of those," said Land. Freedom of expression, Land said, "does not mean freedom to assault the public airwaves or to use telephone lines to transmit offensive cable programming." Tom Minnery, vice president of public policy for Focus on the Family, agreed in the week following the election. "Whatever the Congress can do to lessen the garbage kids are exposed to would be a wonderful advance," he said. "That's what makes Tuesday's election such a sweet victory for conservatives; Michael Moore and his Hollywood pals have been sent packing. That indicates the public's growing distaste for Hollywood values."

On the local level in central Florida, which had just helped send Republican Mel Martinez to occupy a formerly Democratic seat in the U.S. Senate, the reaction to the election results was similar: greater expectations. Rev. Steve Smith, spokesperson for First Baptist Church of Orlando, said Bush's election and his support among conservative Christians showed large portions of the electorate are "grounded in traditional family values." On abortion, for example, "there's no question" there would be pressure from Christian conservatives to appoint judges who "value the sanctity of human life," Smith said. Conservative groups would continue to push for an end to abortion or, at the very least, legislation "greatly limiting" the practice. Paul Scroggins, the executive director of the Christian networking organization Vision Orlando, said social and cultural matters important to evangelicals might become more of a priority for all lawmakers if the group continues to flex its political muscle at the polls. "I think many evangelicals in the past have been either too busy or too apathetic or even too lazy to get involved. I sense though that people now have a greater understanding of their responsibility—a willingness to express those convictions through voting." Erwin McManus, the Los Angeles author and pastor who was in Orlando the weekend after the election to speak at a Promise Keepers rally, said the president "does establish a cultural context, the values he personifies and the values he communicates. He has tremendous influence on cultural norms."

Despite the postelection blustering of some leaders, grass-roots evangelicals I spoke with felt more relieved than triumphant about the results. Going into the campaign, their great fear was that state legislatures in more liberal parts of the country, backed by the federal judiciary and, possibly, future U.S. Congresses, might enact changes in the law antithetical to their beliefs. Evangelicals may not realistically expect to impose their values on the entire nation, if only because they know they can't (despite blue-state panic). Yet they have been quite willing and able—through state and local actions—to impose them on their friends and neighbors. In their minds, however, these are simply defensive maneuvers: they are merely preserving their views on

gay marriage and adoption, abortion and parental notification, absti-
nence education, public nudity in the arts, banning and restricting
books in public libraries and school reading lists, and intervening to
prevent euthanasia.

In a similar vein, there were some voices on the national level that
urged caution, if not magnanimity, in the evangelicals' electoral victory. Charles Colson, former Nixon adviser who later founded Prison
Fellowship, said the president "has a moral mandate, clearly" but cau-
tioned against going too far. "Evangelicals should not be triumphal,"
he said. "I don't view this election as signaling a sudden change in
American culture, or settling all the issues. It's strictly a window of
opportunity." In the days and weeks following the election, Colson
returned to this theme in newspaper and magazine columns and in his
syndicated radio program, *Breakpoint*. In the February 2005 issue of
Christianity Today, he wrote, "Some leaders say that since we're now
in power, we get to impose our will on everyone else—an attitude
repugnant to democratic governance." To think that way, he wrote in
an "Open Letter to the Christian Church," "demeans the Christian
movement . . . I resent the media implication that Christians are waiting for their payback. We're interested in the common good for all
people (the theological term for that is common grace). . . . Let's show
our faith, not by flexing our political muscles, but by our good works."

In the months immediately following the election, the yields were
decidedly mixed for evangelicals. The effort to emasculate the judicial filibuster was thwarted, at least initially, by a group of fourteen
moderate senators from both parties who worked out an uneasy compromise aimed at avoiding a bruising floor battle, a deal that did not
please more hard-line evangelical leaders. The apparent defection of
the National Association of Evangelicals on greenhouse gas emissions (discussed in chapter 5) was another disappointment, as was the
U.S. Supreme Court decision on the Ten Commandments. John
Roberts's appointment to become associate justice and then chief justice was greeted with muted enthusiasm. One group, the Christian
Defense Coalition, released a statement saying it was "difficult for
activists to get excited" about Roberts, with the organization's director, Rev. Patrick Murphy, adding, his hope that "the next nominee will
not have to be a 'stealth' candidate." His fear was largely realized by
the short-lived appointment of Harriet Miers, which conservative and

religious groups "shanghaied," in the words of Pennsylvania Senator Arlen Specter, chair of the Judiciary Committee. By contrast, Bush's nomination of Samuel Alito was well received by these groups, almost to the point of ecstasy. Senate majority leader Bill Frist's defection on stem-cell research was seen as another betrayal, one that prompted James Dobson to compare stem-cell research to Nazi experiments in World War II concentration camps. To the delight of antiabortion activists, Federal Drug Administration Commissioner Lester Crawford ignored the advice of his own scientific advisers and went back on a pledge to several U.S. senators, delaying a decision on the sale of a "morning after" birth control pill. This provoked the head of the agency's Office of Women's Health to resign; this was followed by Crawford's own resignation.

There were some bright spots for evangelicals. On November 30, 2005, the newly appointed chair of the FCC, Kevin J. Martin, said at a forum held before the Senate Commerce Committee, "Parents need better and more tools to help them navigate the entertainment waters, particularly cable and satellite TV." Martin was urging the large cable and satellite companies to offers their channels "a la carte," including a "family friendly" bundle, which the companies have said would be too expensive to do. If they refused, Martin implied that regulators would consider imposing federal decency standards for the pay services. That proved unnecessary. Industry giants Time Warner, Comcast, Cablevision, DirecTV, and EchoStar quickly rolled out "family tier" packages for these values viewers, although some drew later congressional ire for not including sports channels like ESPN. Others at the all-day hearing, including representatives of the Christian Coalition, urged senators to raise the fine for broadcasting indecency from $32,000 per incident to $500,000 per incident. Actions like this prompted some grumbling about the role of evangelicals from within the Republican Party. John Danforth, a former United States senator and United Nations ambassador, himself an Episcopal priest and self-described evangelical, wrote in a *New York Times* Op-Ed column that his party's traditional agenda of reducing the deficit had "become secondary to the agenda of Christian conservatives," who are focused on issues like gay marriage. "By a series of recent initiatives, Republicans have transformed our party into the political arm of conservative Christians." Some wondered whether the evangelicals, having reached a high-water mark in their influence within the GOP, might be overreaching.

Amid what they perceived to be the debacle of the 2004 election, Democrats wondered if there was any way they could stop a resurgent Republican Party—with evangelicals at its helm—from dooming them to long-term minority status. After the postelection controversy involving the National Association of Evangelicals, the *New York Times*'s Elizabeth Bumiller turned to the University of Akron's John Green for his analysis of what two important developments—the environmental controversy involving the NAE and the Calvin College controversy—might signify for the GOP in the mid- to long term. "Were this movement to continue to grow it could create some problems, probably not for President Bush but for future Republican candidates," he told her, in a May 23, 2005, "White House Letter." "Democrats have an opportunity to get some votes." The initial signs were not promising. The Pew Center poll of 2,000 Americans in July of 2005 found that the percentage of those responding who believed that the Democratic Party was "friendly toward religion" had dropped from 40 percent the previous year to 29 percent. Luis E. Lugo told Laurie Goodstein of the *New York Times* on August 31 that "this is a continuation of the Republican Party's very successful use of the values issue in the 2004 election, and the Democrats not being able up until now to answer that successfully."

Some political strategists suggested the solution was deceptively simple, given a look at the recent past, the successful campaigns of Bill Clinton and Jimmy Carter. That is, find a popular Democratic politician in the Sunbelt or the heartland who can carry his own state and perhaps one other in the region and who demonstrate a sincere commitment to Christian faith. Peeling away even a small percentage of evangelicals—those Rick Warren refers to as "Reluctant Republicans"—in traditionally close states like Ohio, Florida, and West Virginia would provide a comfortable electoral college margin. In Ohio in 2004, Bush carried the 25 percent of voters who called themselves born-again Christians or evangelicals by a 3-1 margin, thanks largely to the presence on the ballot of a constitutional amendment banning gay marriage.

"The Democrats have missed their opportunity over and over again," said Los Angeles evangelist Erwin McManus, author of *The*

Barbarian Way: Unleash the Untamed Faith Within (Nashville: Nelson Books, 2005). "The proof has always been right in front of them: Bill Clinton—Southern Baptist; Al Gore—Southern Baptist; and Jimmy Carter—Southern Baptist. Candidates in this mold don't need to reach out to evangelicals, so much as just not alienate them. Reasonable restraint and thoughtful debate would open the doors to evangelicals to consider new political alliances."

Of course, it's not really that simple, especially in the absence of such a deft politician as Clinton, or any prospect of a similar candidate. Part of the problem is Democratic political calculus, as Michael Cromartie of the Ethics and Public Policy Center has pointed out. Clinton's pollster, Stanley Greenberg, has called secular voters the "true loyalists" of the party, the numerical equivalent of white evangelical Protestants in the GOP—about 15 percent of the base. In an article titled "Our Secularist Democratic Party," in the Fall 2002 issue of *The Public Interest,* Louis Bolee and Gerald DeMaio, both political scientists at New York's Baruch College, argue that the Democratic Party has become the home of nonbelievers. In any event, polls agree that the more often Americans attend religious services, the more likely they are to vote Republican. Thus white evangelical Protestants and white observant Roman Catholics— groups that widely supported Bush in 2000 and 2004—are considered largely monolithic blocs in the GOP camp. However, the editorial board of the influential evangelical journal *Books & Culture: A Christian Review* was so divided over the 2004 election that it ran a cover story with the headline "Bono for President." Studies by various pollsters like John Green suggest that Democrats may in fact be able to peel away small numbers of these voters—15–25 percent—known as the "swing faithful." The way to do this, observers think, is to focus their campaigns as much as possible on economic issues and to steer the discussion away from volatile social, cultural, and theological issues. Democratic candidates such as Carter and Clinton perfected this approach: Speak what experts call the "language of the faith"—with a Southern accent if possible—while appealing to voters' economic interests.

Orlando attorney Aubrey Ducker fits the profile of the swing faithful. An evangelical Southern Baptist and, until 2000, a registered Republican, he supported Kerry in 2004. He opposed the Iraq war and the Bush administration's tax cuts, which some evangelical supporters say is a religious issue. "I'm embarrassed that any Christian would look at taxes and tax relief as a religious issue," said Ducker, thirty-six, in a pre-election interview. "It's not." Even with Bush's 50,000-vote victory over Kerry in Florida in 2004, it would not take many voters such as Ducker to cause a seismic shift in the electoral college. Catholics are also part of the swing faithful. Bob Dellecker, a forty-five-year-old Orlando attorney, told me for the same *Orlando Sentinel* story that he thought neither Bush nor Kerry had "a fully Catholic position" on all the issues. "I can't divorce myself from domestic or foreign policy," he said. "A single issue does not determine my vote with these two candidates. They're both a mixed bag. That's what makes this election so difficult."

Other evangelicals are already committed Democrats. Kristen Millson and Amanda March both work at the child development center at All Saints Episcopal Church in Winter Park, and both consistently vote Democratic. Not that it's easy supporting their party's candidates. Each told me the same anecdote, about an older woman at the congregation who was a vigorous Kerry backer in 2004, her car plastered with bumper stickers like one that read, "God told me to vote for John Kerry." While she was parked in front of the parish office, nails were driven into all of her tires, and a key was used to make a long scratch in the paint. "I think there's some hostility there," said Millson, thirty-seven, the daughter of a moderately Republican college professor. "As a Democrat, I know I am a minority."

Nonetheless, the mother of three put a Kerry sticker on her car and was delighted when people at her school would come up to whisper that she was not alone. Others took one look at the vehicle and suggested that she needed more Bible study. For a Democratic candidate to make headway among her persuadable friends, Millson said, "You'd have to find someone moderate enough in their fiscal policy who wouldn't scare those people away." Millson, who has been in a number of Christian mothers' groups at her church, said her support for Democrats is rooted in her faith, despite the disapproval of other congregation members. "I felt pretty alienated at church. It is pretty irritating to me for people to assume that we all believe the same thing. We're Christians, too. We want to worship with like-minded theological conservatives, but on social issues we have a different view of what we should be doing. Jesus' teachings were quite liberal, socially."

March, forty-seven, has been on numerous mission trips and has participated in many Bible and religious study groups, and considers herself moderately liberal on theological issues. A strong opponent of the Iraq war and the death penalty, she said it is sometimes actually painful to talk about her politics to other members at All Saints, where she has been a member for thirty years. She has strongly held views on environmentalism, education, and health care, and she has no problem with increasing taxation to pay for programs that help those in need. "I used to be reluctant to talk about my political positions. Now it's impossible for me not to talk about them." She had no Kerry stickers on her car in 2004, but she did have lawn signs supporting the Massachusetts senator in her Maitland neighborhood. She was a "huge fan" of Bill Clinton in 1992 and liked John Edwards in the early going of the 2004 primary season. But she said she fears that a Democratic candidate would almost need to appear to be a fundamentalist in order to carry central Florida's nationally crucial Interstate 4 corridor.

National Democratic strategists believe that values are as important as faith in appealing to more liberal evangelical voters. Barbara Dafoe Whitehead, writing for the magazine of the centrist Democratic Leadership Council, suggested a family-values-oriented form of populism, one that clearly echoed Bill Clinton.

> Any good populist appeal begins by identifying with the worth and dignity of Americans who work hard, play by the rules, and thereby make the nation stronger and better. . . . Side with the people against the powerful interests is populism. But what makes it progressive is the core belief that rearing children is not just a private responsibility for parents to bear alone. The public has an interest—and the state has a role—in supporting parents and in leveling the playing field.

The goal of these changes is certainly worth it, progressive evangelicals say. Speaking to the Texas Faith Network, a liberal religious organization, James C. Moore, co-author of *Bush's Brain: How Karl Rove Made George Bush Presidential,* put it this way: "If ever there was a bleeding-heart liberal, it was Jesus Christ. I think the carpenter from Galilee was the original Democrat."

Jim Wallis, of *Sojourners* magazine and community, traveled the nation during the 2004 campaign in a bus dubbed "Call to Renewal." His Washington-based community—which describes itself as "a progressive Christian commentary on faith, politics and culture"—took out newspaper ads reading, "God is not a Republican or a Democrat." Though ostensibly nonpartisan, Wallis said, his group was "challenging our friends on the religious right," who were focusing their efforts solely on issues such as gay marriage, an approach he said was "outrageous." Moral issues must include war and peace, the death penalty, nuclear weapons, the environment, and economic justice, Wallis said. "The Republican Party is not 'God's Own Party,' as the religious right and some Republican leaders seem to be suggesting," he wrote in the May 11, 2005, issue of *Sojourners* online newsletter. "And of course, neither is the Democratic Party. We must say it again and again until it is heard and understood: God is not partisan; God is not a Republican or a Democrat. When either party tries to politicize God, or co-opt religious communities for its political agenda, it makes a terrible mistake. God's politics challenge all our politics. Our faith must not be narrowed to the agenda of one political party."

Nor should it be excluded from any party. Since the election and the publication of his book *God's Politics: Why the Right Gets It Wrong and the Left Doesn't Get It: A New Vision for Faith and Politics in America* Wallis has been lecturing Democrats on how to reach "values voters." In an interview in the April 2005 issue of *Christianity Today,* Wallis explained the kind of advice he was giving. Democrats, he said,

> have ceded the territory of religion and moral values to the Republican side, and it has been defined in very partisan ways. Religion and values get used as wedges to divide people and not bridges to pull us together. I tell Democrats three things: First, reframe policy issues in the values context. Start with values and talk about how policies flow from values. Second, reconnect with the constituencies you're disconnected from, which means listening to people who aren't listening to you. And, third, rethink some of the big issues: economy, security, abortion, family.

The most challenging of these may be modifying the party core's absolutist position on abortion. "It's important for the Democrats to change the way they talk about abortion, to respect pro-life Democrats," Wallis told the magazine. "You've got to talk about some reasonable restrictions. Waiting periods and late-term abortion restrictions." Such suggestions have drawn criticism from Barry Lynn of Americans United for the Separation of Church and State. Wallis was not dissuaded, and for good reason. "What's at stake is the meaning of being an evangelical," he told about nine hundred members of First Congregational Church in Pasadena, California, according to the March 28, 2005, *Los Angeles Times.* "The monologue of the religious right is over, and a new dialogue has begun!"

As John Green's research strongly suggests, there is a significant progressive minority among evangelicals on a variety of issues, a fact sometimes obscured when religious voters are given only two choices in an election. There is also a much smaller, distinctly radical—and, I would say, redemptive—minority of evangelical leaders whose interest extends well beyond partisan politics. While Jim Wallis may be the best known nationally, there are others, like Rev. Jim Ball, founder of the Evangelical Environmental Network, and Ron Sider, head of Evangelicals for Social Action. The author of *Rich Christians in an Age of Hunger* and *The Scandal of the Evangelical Conscience,* and secretary of Evangelicals for McGovern in 1972, Sider is particularly concerned with hypocrisy. In another *Christianity Today* interview, he said, "Precisely at a time when evangelicals have more political power to raise the issue of moral values in the society than they've had in a long time, the hard statistics on their own living show that they don't live what they're talking about." In *The Scandal of the Evangelical Conscience,* he wrote, "Whether the issue is divorce, materialism, sexual promiscuity, racism, physical abuse in marriage, or neglect of a biblical worldview, the polling data point to widespread, blatant disobedience on the part of people who allegedly are evangelical, born-again Christians. The statistics are devastating."

Tony Campolo, a fiery Baptist evangelist and author, is at least as outspoken in his articulation of a radical social gospel, including opposition to the death penalty. "Evangelicals and the Religious Right are seen as synonymous and that is to the detriment of our ministry," he told England's *Baptist Times* in April of 2005. "After the election, we have come across as anti-gay, anti-woman, pro-war, pro-guns and indifferent to the poor," he said. "Is that what evangelical Christianity is all about?" I know both the voluble Campolo and the taciturn Wallis and admire both men immensely. But how many evangelicals they and Sider and others represent is difficult to gauge; it may not be numerically significant. Joe Loconte, a fellow at the conservative Heritage Foundation, wrote in an Op-Ed column for the July 1, 2005, *Wall Street Journal* that such men have "no obvious grassroots constituency," and he may be right. Wallis replied in his online *Sojourners* newsletter that on his most recent national book tour he found "a silent majority of moderate and progressive people who don't feel represented by the shrill tones and ideological agenda of the Religious Right, nor the disdainful attitudes toward religion from the secular left." Whatever their strength, the influence of these socially conscious thinkers on younger evangelicals may be another matter. Glenn Palmberg, president of the 110,000-member Evangelical Covenant Church, a Chicago-based denomination, told the *Los Angeles Times* that Wallis "is giving voice to a sizable number of open-minded evangelicals who say we don't like what is happening to the word 'evangelical.' We don't like abortion, but we see the connection to poverty. A lot of people are opposed to gay marriage, but we don't see this as a threat to our marriage and have gay friends. Poverty and war are huge issues. We're not one- or two-issue voters."

An aspiring young politician from Orlando whom I met while doing a story on "God and Man at Harvard" suggested a way Democrats might bridge the faith and values gap in the future.

Chapter 7

God and Man at Harvard

A Chris among the Pagans

In early 1999, the *Sentinel* dispatched me to Harvard to do a story about a local student named Chris King, who had just been the center of a campus controversy in Cambridge. I suspected that the assignment was no coincidence—his family lived next door to my publisher, on a lake in Winter Park, a fashionable town adjoining Orlando. With a prominent and successful attorney father, and a health care executive and community activist mother, Chris's life had been informed by affluence. But I later learned it was also touched by tragedy; during Chris's freshman year at Harvard his oldest brother, David, who was gay, committed suicide. The tragedy rocked the whole family.

The Harvard experience itself had been a culture shock for Chris. In stark contrast to central Florida, he was immersed in an academic community where Jews are strongly represented among the student body and faculty, along with mainline Protestants, Catholics, Hindus, Muslims, Buddhists, as well as no small number of skeptics, agnostics, and atheists. Thus, as an evangelical Christian, Chris was in the minority in Cambridge, something made plain to him from his first week at school at a student project aimed at acquainting freshman with the Boston community. Among the first of several hundred students gathered in an off-campus basement, he recalled introducing himself this way: "Hi, I'm Chris King from Winter Park, Florida, and I am excited about getting involved in one of the Christian outreach ministries on campus." Afterwards, a junior came up and congratulated him for his bravery, which puzzled him. From that point on, he later wrote, "I would be forced to focus on who I was as a person of faith, and what that would look and feel like in this new environment." Not that there wouldn't be bright spots. Chris spent a semester in one of Harvard's most celebrated courses, a seminar taught by Dr. Armand Nicholi, created as a theoretical dialogue between two towering intellects of the twentieth century, the Christian C. S. Lewis and the atheist Sigmund Freud. Chris studied under Peter Gomes, the charismatic author and Harvard chaplain, whom the young student called "one of the most articulate defenders of the Gospel I have ever met." When Billy Graham came through Boston one fall semester, Chris was selected to read the Scriptures that the evangelist used as his sermon text. Harvard also introduced the student to Jim Wallis, the evangelical activist who was a visiting professor at Harvard's Divinity School and Kennedy School of Government, whom we have encountered elsewhere in this book. Like the progressive evangelist Tony Campolo, Wallis believes in a religious faith that can change things in this world. Chris later told me that he saw Wallis as his mentor, taking his course, "Faith, Politics and Public Policy," and spending the summer of 1999 at Wallis's inner-city community, Sojourners.

The incident that sent me to Cambridge in 1999 was that Chris, then a twenty-year-old sophomore, believed that he had lost a close race for president of Harvard's student government council because of religious prejudice. In December, after a campaign to build community values on the campus, he was defeated by 100 votes—out of 3,000 total cast for 10 candidates. The loss, he said, was the result of "sophisticated slander," which had effectively portrayed King and his supporters as religious zealots running a stealth campaign to seize power. His campaign, which had been attracting good crowds to its rallies, was doomed, King said, "once they found out the simple fact that I was a Christian." Efforts against him included fliers that said he wanted to evangelize other students and an editorial in the campus newspaper that raised concern about his ties to religious groups. But King's loss, the family's minister said, provided a good lesson for the young man. "I don't think he's been treated badly," said Rev. Howard Edington, then pastor of First Presbyterian Church of Orlando, the influential downtown congregation where his family had long worshiped. "He had to stand for what he believes, and he did it in what I believe is a courageous manner. That he didn't win is almost immaterial to me. His inner strength is going to make a difference."

Others at Harvard insisted that the affair had been blown out of proportion and were worried about the implication that the historically liberal school may have shown the very intolerance it abhorred in other areas of society. King's religion was only one of several factors that led to his defeat, they said, and a minor one at that. "It's convenient for him to interpret himself as being a victim of some sort of anti-Christian bias," said Noah Oppenheim of Tucson, Arizona, editorial chair and columnist for the campus newspaper, the *Harvard Crimson.* "Whereas in reality he's just another kid who lost a student-government election." Some elements of this tale of God and man at Harvard were not in dispute. The university has a reputation for liberalism and secularism, and when I visited the campus, I saw few announcements for religious organizations on bulletin boards. But Archie C. Epps III, longtime dean of students, said that he noticed a rise in the number of religious students. "I predict a growing influence of practicing believers in college life," he said. "The evangelical movement has made a breakthrough into the public debate at Harvard." Epps, who died in 2003, was prophetic—Chris was in fact in the vanguard of a much larger movement. The following year, the woman who ran unsuccessfully for vice president of student government on Chris's ticket was elected president by more than 700 votes. In April of 2005 an active Christian was elected student body president at Dartmouth.

A front-page article in the May 22, 2005, *New York Times* detailed the successful efforts of evangelical Christians to find a home for themselves at Ivy League universities, beginning with Princeton, Brown, and Cornell. Two Dallas, Texas, brothers, Matt and Monty Bennett, both with ties to Orlando-based Campus Crusade for Christ, had founded an organization called Christian Union. The purpose of the organization, the *Times's* Laurie Goodstein and David D. Kirkpatrick wrote, was to create a "beachhead of evangelicals in the American elite," at universities like Brown, which "was founded by Protestant ministers as an expressly Christian college. But over the years it gradually shed its religious affiliation and became a secular institution, as did the other Ivies." The goal of the Christian Union, according to its fundraising materials, is to "reclaim the Ivy League for Christ," and to "shape the hearts and minds of many thousands who graduate from these schools and who become the elites in other American cultural institutions," according to the *Times.*

However, Chris King's goals were much more modest—and personal—when we met at Harvard. I found him handsome, gifted, and articulate as we strolled the campus, stopping to chat at length for my *Sentinel* story. But what struck me most was the paradox of his situation. Chris strongly believed that being a Christian was a political liability in his student government run. But in central Florida, *not* being an evangelical Christian could be at least as crippling a political handicap. In Sunbelt cities such as Orlando, personal faith and church membership are tremendous, almost requisite, political advantages, as Chris acknowledged. He credited his prominent role in the Fellowship of Christian Athletes, where he frequently shared his beliefs with groups of students, for helping him win election after election for student government at Winter Park High School. However, more cynical (and less visibly religious) students also grumbled about his slickness. But his faith-based social conscience was manifest in other ways in high school. Chris created a program to provide free junior prom tickets, and financial aid for dresses and tuxes, for cash-strapped students. When the family of another classmate, an African American woman, was evicted from their home, Chris offered her a room in his own home until another place could be found.

"Faith came easily, and it was nurtured by a community who encouraged me at every step," he recalled in a July 3, 2005, essay for the *Sentinel.* "I had been raised by a family who placed great importance on my spiritual life," he wrote. King said his life was changed one summer when, as a teenager, he attended a Christian summer leadership camp in Georgia. "I was inspired to live in a way that was not just for me but was glorifying my God," he recalled. The young man took this faith with him to Cambridge, attending the Memorial Church on the Harvard campus on Sundays and joining a prayer and Bible study group called Christian Impact. The prayer group, which involved about fifty students, had its roots in Campus Crusade for Christ but was not formally affiliated with the Orlando-based organization, because of university regulations. National organizations that are in any way considered exclusive are prohibited on the Harvard campus. Outside of his prayer group, King kept a lower religious profile than he did in Florida, where he frequently gave testimony of his Christian faith.

But at Harvard, the former basketball star found no home-court advantage for Christians. When he launched his campaign for president of Harvard's undergraduate student council, Chris made no reference to his religion. Although members of his prayer group were at the core of his campaign, his platform spoke only to the community's shared values, chiefly "compassion, collaboration and innovation." He deliberately included gay students in his campaign. One of their goals, "building a healthier Harvard," echoed a campaign led by Chris's mother, Marilyn, called the Healthy Community Initiative of Greater Orlando. That effort, a long-term program for change, was "designed to bring together a diverse group of citizens to forge a shared vision for our community," Marilyn King said, mostly through meetings, forums, workshops, and discussions. At Winter Park High, she said, "Chris always had a real diverse group of friends. He's always been extraordinarily concerned about people and about trying to make a difference," including work for organizations such as the Coalition for the Homeless.

King's campaign—his effort to make a difference at Harvard—was disrupted when an e-mail surfaced, sent by a woman serving on the student government's election commission to fellow members of the Harvard-Radcliffe Christian Fellowship. Margaret White wrote that her position on the commission—which ensures fairness in student elections— required her to remain "officially neutral" among the candidates. Nonetheless, she then went on to ask her friends to pray for King and his running mate "for their protection from Satan's tactics to undermine their confidence in doing His work. . . . I know that God's hand is directing them to run, as it has been directing them for so long." When news of the e-mail created a controversy, White resigned from the commission. King told the *Crimson* that he had not asked for her support or for that of the Harvard-Radcliffe Christian Fellowship. Still, with the e-mail, the issue of King's religion had entered the campaign. Days later, anonymous leaflets appeared on the doors of freshman dorms, alleging that the King campaign was a vehicle to evangelize "non-believing students."

King was stunned by the fabrication. "People knew how to put words together to trigger certain fears," he said, "and that's what happened." He was shocked again when he read the *Crimson* editorial that endorsed the eventual winner, a conservative Republican who focused on such nuts-and-bolts issues as having dorms wired for cable television. The same editorial dismissed the King campaign's call for "values-driven leadership" as vague and unrelated to the mundane, housekeeping responsibilities of student government. The paper added, "Their ties to religious groups have raised concerns among many students." Josh Simon of Palm Beach Gardens, Florida, president of the *Crimson,* insisted that the paper's choice was not based on the fact that King was religious, although he acknowledged that "I can see how people might interpret it that way." Another factor in King's defeat, Simon said, was that several weeks before the election, King had joined one of Harvard's exclusive all-male social clubs. This seemed hypocritical to some voters in light of the King campaign's emphasis on "inclusion" Simon said. Like others at Harvard, Simon was reluctant to read anything larger into King's defeat, and he dismissed charges of religious discrimination. The anonymous flier, Simon said, was "definitely a reflection of what goes on on the national level in terms of how campaigns are run."

Dean Epps condemned the flier and the bad feeling it generated among King's supporters and others on the campus. "We want to find some way to signal to students that we think a strong religious life is a good thing," Epps said. Such a signal might have been necessary. King's defeat was the subject of a critical Op-Ed column in the *Wall Street Journal* and a commentary on Christian radio by Charles Colson. The lesson of the election, said the Southern Baptist Convention's Rev. Richard Land, himself a Princeton graduate, was clear. "If you are overtly religious, or if you can be made out to be overtly religious," he said, "then that is supposed to disqualify you from the eligibility to hold office."

But King declined to be pigeonholed when I interviewed him in 1999. "I don't want to be a poster boy for the Christian Coalition," he said, noting that he was a Democrat and admirer of former U.S. Senator Bill Bradley. Jerry Falwell and others, he said, offered a message "painted with the brush of intolerance and unkindness. How are you going to share your faith with someone if you've alienated and intimidated them?" It was clear to me then that Chris King was planning a career in public service, undaunted by his Harvard political experience. In order to understand the meaning of what happened—and to make sure it didn't happen again—he created his own undergraduate curriculum that enabled him to study religion, government, and public policy at the Kennedy School of Government and the Divinity School, as well as at the undergraduate college.

Chris graduated from Harvard in June of 2001, "with my faith intact and strengthened by the challenges I faced," he wrote in his 2005 *Sentinel* essay.

I could not have done it without a praying family and a God who I found out did not just reside in Orlando, Florida, but was also very much alive in Cambridge, Massachusetts. . . . It is a fact that people of faith are fewer at Harvard, but it is wrong to think that Harvard and other Ivy League schools are not places where people of faith and ideas inspired by faith reside and thrive. . . . Certainly I faced some challenges while I was there, but I also recognize that Harvard was a place that opened my mind and heart to a higher level of thinking. . . . My time at Harvard was all about faith and navigating its appropriate role in my friendships, my studies, and my campus activities. It was my personal challenge, just as I believe it is becoming the defining challenge of our country on a national level. We are a nation divided on the issues central to faith and politics.

The issues are thorny and the entrenched ideologies offer little hope for common ground, but as I consider how I will approach these social issues, I frequently look back on my time at Harvard. Harvard taught me that language is so important. People are repelled or attracted by language, and when we pay little heed to how we say what we believe, we devalue what we believe and the One we are serving. Second, Harvard showed me that people of faith have to be civil. The ends never justify the means. When we disagree with another person, we must refrain from demonizing them. Too often the debate is less about who is right or wrong, than about who is good and evil. That logic may win political contests, but if my limited experience is any guide, it is not sustainable. . . . Finally, Harvard impressed upon me that people of faith must aspire to apply their faith to all the issues, not just a few. When we are morally selective, our personal statement and the way we are received by people who come from different faith traditions or no faith tradition is compromised.

I learned these lessons the hard way. I learned them at a place that has a habit of applying scrutiny to people of faith. But that scrutiny can be a good thing; the scrutiny I faced allowed me to test my faith in a hostile environment and develop a more winsome way of communicating it. My experience forced me to learn what makes many people apprehensive of Christians, and it left me with a feeling of responsibility to always be sensitive to those fears. From my first day at Harvard to my last, I feel assured that everything happened for a reason.

In 1999 Chris King told me he was also looking ahead to law school. My sense, from my political reporting days, was that if he chose an Ivy League law school, that would indicate that his goal was the federal judiciary. If he decided on the University of Florida, it would mean a return to the state and to a career in electoral politics. After graduation, he headed for Gainesville, and by 2005 he had graduated from law school, married, and was studying for the bar exam. After that, he planned to join his father's Orlando firm. I called him and asked if he was still a Democrat, and he said he was. In an e-mail, I also asked him about a whole range of issues. But first I wanted to know why he was still a Democrat.

"Why am I a Democrat?" he asked. "I'm a Democrat because I believe government has a responsibility to reduce inequality, increase opportunity, foster diversity, and build a more civil society. The Democratic Party at its best aspires to further each of these goals ... goals that are rooted in Judeo-Christian values and goals that mirror my own values." Out of political prudence, I suppose, he begged off answering the queries about third-rail issues like abortion, gay marriage, the death penalty, civil unions, and, specifically, about Iraq. The closest he came on the war was in his response to my question about working with multinational organizations. "I believe strongly in the value of multilateral thinking," he wrote, "from coordinating international aid missions and peace-keeping attempts to fostering multilateral organizations like the United Nations, an internationalist worldview is in the best interest of America's finances and security and a key tool in resolving conflicts peaceably."

Religion threaded through some of his other answers, which basically echoed centrist positions articulated by the Democratic Leadership Council:

Environment: "We have a God-given mandate to protect and celebrate the environment. I believe that the environmental impact of all major government initiatives should be considered, studied, and valued in policy making. We should continue to strive to keep America's waters, parks, and air sustainable for future generations."

Deficit and economic policy: "I believe America's economic policymakers should aspire to balance the federal budget. We should not as a rule spend more that we have, and then pass the debt on to future generations. Wars and national disasters can occasionally disrupt our ability to balance the budget, but fiscal responsibility should encourage a return to balancing the budget at the earliest possible time."

Stem-cell research: "I support stem-cell research and believe that government should partner with private organizations and universities to extend the reach and impact of this promising research on behalf of all those suffering from debilitating diseases that may one day have a cure."

Affirmative action: "I strongly oppose quotas, but I do support Affirmative Action as it has been defined by the U.S. Supreme Court. I believe in the law that allows universities to consider the diversity of its applicants—ranging from socio-economic diversity to racial diversity to academic interest diversity—in their admissions decisions. I believe that fostering diversity in our nation's universities should be a significant goal."

Chris and I met later in the café area of a Barnes & Noble not far from downtown, sitting at a small round table. Since last we spoke, Chris had won a state mock-trial competition, taken the bar exam, bought a house in a gentrifying downtown neighborhood, and was finishing his first week as a civil litigator at his father's firm. Understandably, he looked tired, in a pink tie loosened at the collar of his white shirt, gray suit pants, black socks, and shoes. What struck me was that he had become even more poised in the six years since I had seen him in Cambridge, his smile still warm and natural. Graceful and comfortable in his skin, almost serene, he wears his self-confidence lightly. One of his gifts, now much more refined, is the ability to put people at ease. "I'm very comfortable with who I am," he told me, not uncomfortable with the way I describe his privileged upbringing in the first paragraph of this chapter. "That's who I am. I had an idyllic childhood and I've had a lot of easy breaks," he said, explaining his deep and ongoing commitment to community and public service, without resort to clichés about noblesse oblige. His brother's death has left him with a palpable and visceral reaction to homophobia, although he said that does not automatically translate into support for any particular item on the "gay political agenda."

I couldn't help wondering if I was sitting across from a twenty-something, upper-middle-class Bill Clinton—or at least the template for a twenty-first-century version. So I asked about his future. "I believe there will be a day when I'll enter politics—but that could be twenty years from now," he told me. Given his electoral experience as a Harvard undergraduate, is he at all concerned about the much less genteel rough-and-tumble of the real-life stump and political arena? "I like to think I can modulate my message, to take complex issues and communicate them in a winsome and compelling way," he said. "Winsome" again? That sounded a little rehearsed to me, but maybe he can make it work.

Orange County and the city of Orlando, with their growing Democratic majorities fueled in part by an influx of Puerto Ricans from the island and New York, would probably offer King numerous opportunities for winnable districts. A congressional seat or a state-wide race may be another matter. For now, he's just a well-spoken, good-looking guy with a nice resume and strong family connections. Whether he can parlay that into a successful political career depends on a number of factors, chiefly what he does between now and when he decides to run. There are also developments beyond his control, like whether the political climate and demography in this part of the Sunbelt shifts toward the center. Or if the Democratic Party label turns out to be a liability.

"The question for Chris and his fellow Democrats is whether they can win an election in the region on anything but personal charisma," said Peter Brown, codirector of the Quinnipiac University Polling Institute and former chief political correspondent for Scripps Howard News Service.

> Bill Clinton is the model. He took enough off the rough edges that white southern Christian voters see in the Democratic Party to finesse his policy positions. Clinton won the support he did in the South because he was many things to many people. He was able to convince enough white Christian voters that he shared their values, if not their views. But he was a once-in-a-lifetime political talent, comparable to a Michael Jordan in his abilities.

It used to be that the up-and-coming political types in the South were all Democrats, but that was another era. There are still white Christians like Chris King, who on paper look to have electoral potential. But when they have to confront the fundamental differences between what their party stands for and what most white Christians in the South believe, they have a political problem. Since pragmatism would lead any ambitious type who lacked strong beliefs to jump off on the GOP side of the fence, those who insist they are Democrats do so out of conviction. But they will have to be as adept as Clinton was in walking that very narrow tightrope. Clinton was able to finesse abortion and to call for a middle-class tax cut, and gay rights was not yet a campaign issue. The Chris Kings of the future will have to be both as adept and as lucky in the political environment to give the Democrats a chance at winning back the region of the country that they once solidly owned.

Linda Chapin, the last Democratic candidate elected across Orange County, who served as county executive, sees King's future differently. "If I believed in 'destiny'—which I don't—I would imagine the hand of fate hovering only briefly over Chris King's cradle before delivering a solid tap on his shoulder," she told me over coffee at a Panera's restaurant just off Orlando's downtown Lake Eola. She had written some of her thoughts about King:

> Never have I encountered anyone, young or old, with so much natural talent for leadership. One of the important elements to his successes, past and future, is that for Chris, the personal is political. While he's intuitively strategic in addressing his goals, he's also entirely values-driven. His unquestioned sincerity and depth are not only surprising in this age of political cynicism, but unusual in today's society, when caring so much can sometimes be perceived as weakness instead of strength. His values, however, have little to do with the overworked "litmus" issues of the current scene; they demonstrate instead a genuine commitment to the democratic process and to people, of all kinds but especially those left behind by the excesses of the past decade.

For the moment, Chapin is out of electoral politics, running a think tank called the Metropolitan Center for Regional Studies at the University of Central Florida. But it is hard for her to rein in her enthusiasm for King, whom she has known since he was a boy:

It's this uniqueness that will serve him in any political climate. But I also believe that there's a big change coming in the partisan landscape, as more citizens move away from adherence to any particular party. The ever-deeper ideological gulf between Republicans and Democrats has left most of us stranded somewhere in the middle, and while this may not develop into a third-party movement, it will lead many voters to look past party labels for someone they can believe in (that impulse is revealed in the remarkable response to youthful Barack Obama, and there will be others). The longing for an authentic voice that can motivate and inspire to action, or even sacrifice, is a response to years of political leadership that is amoral at worst, calculated and cynical at best. If we're really lucky, Chris King and other young people like him will take us into a new era of reform and renewal.

Chapter 8

Confronting Popular Culture

Consider the Alternatives

*I*n states across the Sunbelt, evangelicals see Republican and largely Christian control of most, if not all, branches of government, from their towns and cities to Washington, D.C. Conservatives dominate their AM radio dials, and the Fox News channel leads the local cable news television ratings. Christian books are a staple of the national bestseller lists. Yet to a great degree evangelicals still feel powerless in the face of an inescapable threat that saturates their environment. And it is a threat they cannot defeat at the polls—a pervasive, inescapable popular culture they consider to be, for the most part, a toxic mix of loveless sexuality and senseless violence.

"Fundamentalists are convinced that pop culture is stealing the souls of their children," Richard Goldstein wrote in the February 21, 2005, issue of *The Nation,* and he is right. One thing I have learned for certain from living and working among evangelicals is that there is a strong consensus among religious people—clergy and lay—on the importance of communicating faith and belief to teens and young adults. Christian leaders want to preserve the faith (and innocence) of their children and, if possible, to reach out to the children of the unchurched. The greatest challenge—and competition—they face in achieving this goal is the temptation of what they believe to be a decadent, nihilistic, secular culture. Yet pastors also recognize a contradiction: those in the pews are desperate to find ways to safely access this undeniably seductive culture, if they can. Youth and parachurch ministries acknowledge that they need to hold and reach young people in middle school, high school, and college before they drift away from their faith. At the same time, lay Christians and their children do not want to be left out of the culture, isolated from their peers or, if you will, "left behind." Yet they do not want to be corrupted by it. "Popularization of the idea of a comprehensive Christian worldview—Christ as Lord of 'every aspect of life'—has increased the legitimacy of evangelical participation in popular culture," wrote William Romanowski of Calvin College in the February 2004 issue of the journal *Perspectives.* "I suggest that a paradigm shift is underway in the evangelical community, as a posture of aversion has shifted to one of engagement."

This discussion is not a new one. In the 1920s, fundamentalists were also ambivalent about popular culture, according to Quentin Schultze, Romanowski's Calvin College colleague. "On the one hand, they criticized newer forms of public entertainment, from vaudeville to film. On the other hand, they believed that religious radio might counter the modernism that allegedly threatened the Christian faith; the airways would serve the church by delivering the gospel to every living human being." Today, American Christians— and in particular the estimated fifty million adult evangelicals—are also grappling with ways to access mass popular culture, by tailoring or filtering secular products or by creating qualitatively competitive, religious alternatives. In particular, they are adapting all the major genres of mass popular culture—books, music, movies, radio, television, comics, video games, high school cheerleading, and even standup comedy, professional wrestling, and theme parks. Halloween, once abhorred by evangelicals, has been appropriated with everything from scary "Hell Houses" warning teens about sex and drugs; to church-based Harvest Festivals for young children, with costumes from the Bible; to mixing sophisticated religious tracts with candy for unsaved trick-or-treaters. "Christians have a great need for entertainment," Bill Anderson, of the Christian Booksellers Association, told Paula Zahn of CNN's *People in the News,* in an interview broadcast on March 28, 2005. "We are not absolved of that human desire for entertainment and escape. . . . There have been some attempts at filling that void, but the void is bigger than the inventory of selection."

According to a July 16, 2001, article in *Newsweek* magazine, by mid-2001, identifiably "Christian" entertainment in various genres was already grossing more than $3 billion annually, a figure now estimated by industry experts at more than four billion dollars. In so doing, Christian entertainment producers have made a discovery. This same popular culture that in their minds can be such a menace may in fact provide an avenue to reach out to people not otherwise inclined to religion. What may have begun as a defensive effort has evolved into a mission, and American religious leaders in increasing numbers are turning to popular culture to communicate their theological values. And they are not satisfied with creating a viable alternative popular culture for other Christians. With the best of their products, they are now extending well beyond the sizable Christian audience, hoping to cross over to a mainstream market. This approach seems to be gaining momentum—although it may best be accomplished through stealth and subterfuge. Perhaps it is because I write a lot about religion and popular culture, or because I live in Orlando, but I see evidence of this phenomenon everywhere. Given the considerable buying power of evangelical consumers, it is not surprising that this constituency was able to fuel the success of Tim LaHaye and Jerry Jenkins's Left Behind series of the novels. But evangelicals alone are not enough of a market to account for the success of Mel Gibson's film *The Passion of the Christ.* (A similar spillover effect is evident in the secular culture, which increasingly includes religious themes, plots, and characters in mainstream popular media.)

For example, the Bible is not the only book evangelical Christians like to read. They also like history, biography, poetry, fantasy and science fiction, and, yes, romance. Christian fiction—religious pulp fiction, especially—has exploded, first in North America, but with ripples throughout the world. Before the March 2004 release of *Glorious Appearing,* the final book in the Left Behind series, 2002's *The Remnant* pushed the cumulative sales total for the series and its spin-offs to more than sixty million copies, rivaling *Harry Potter.* Advance printings of *Glorious Appearing* were in excess of two million copies. These potboiler novels, whose authors claim are based on the book of Revelation, continue to sell and spin off others. LaHaye's successor series, for which he has received a multimillion-dollar advance, is based on a Christian archeologist who sounds a lot like Steven Spielberg's screen hero Indiana Jones. The first of these, *Babylon Rising,* sold more than 300,000 copies in its first six months. Frank Peretti has also had success with novels ranging from *This Present*

Darkness to *Hangman's Curse,* which was subsequently made into a feature film, then released on DVD and broadcast nationally on the ABC Family Network just before Halloween in 2004. Thomas Nelson, a Nashville-based religious publisher that is also the world's ninth-largest publisher, is a leader in the field. "We publish all kinds of fiction—suspense, science fiction and romance—with no explicit sex or violence and written from a Christian perspective," Rebeca DeBoard, a Nelson publicist, told the *Orlando Sentinel*'s book editor, Nancy Pate, in a March 30, 2004, article. "What we've found is that people are looking for really good stories with substance and values." Nelson's fiction subsidiary, WestBow, had the distinction of publishing the first Christian "chick-lit" novel, *What a Girl Wants,* by Kristin Billerbeck. The lighthearted tale about a cute single Christian lawyer "with absolutely adorable shoes" was released in March of 2003. A sequel, *She's Out of Control,* appeared in August of 2004. "The character always has to slow down and hear what God is saying to them," Billerbeck told a conference of Christian romance writers in Denver, according to a September 21, 2004, article in the *New York Times.* Similar WestBow books, like *Savannah from Savannah* and *Savannah Comes Undone* by Denise Hildreth, followed. In the latter, Savannah's mother chains herself to a Ten Commandments monument, a comic episode the publisher characterizes as "hysterical." Nelson published another novel in the same genre, *The Yada Yada Prayer Group,* by Nada Jackson, which sold more than 75,000 copies, according to the *Times.* "The Christian Booksellers Association estimates that total sales of Christian fiction have topped $2 billion a year," wrote Joshua Kurlantzick, "and the market share of Christian romance has grown 25 percent a year since 2001, the Evangelical Christian Publishers Association reported." Christian denominational presses, from the Southern Baptists to the Mormons, have released their own lines of fiction, just as commercial publishers have purchased or established subsidiaries to do the same. The Southern Baptists' publisher, Broadman & Holman, had a hit with *Mission Compromised,* a thriller by former Iran-Contra figure, radio talk-show host, and Fox commentator Oliver North. "It's covert in its message and in its content and story line," said John Thompson, the company's vice president of marketing. "But it's also covert in the sense that it offers a clear message of hope through Jesus

Christ. In the sense that the main characters are not Christians in the beginning of the book, but they do come to that. More importantly, it clearly presents the Gospel." The Mormons' first entry was *Lords of Perdition,* by Warren Fast, a science-fiction adventure story about warriors who protect the earth from demons, which, like the Left Behind novels, claims to be based on the book of Revelation. To capitalize on the rise of Christian romance novels, Harlequin Books, a commercial house which publishes romance fiction, in 1996 established Steeple Hill division, where there is no cursing and all the sex takes place within marriage and behind closed doors.

The evangelism represented by these books can be direct as well as indirect. Christian publishers have donated tens of thousands of titles to jails and prisons across the nation, many distributed through the Prison Book Project in Titusville, Florida, founded by Ray Hill. The retired aerospace worker told Laurin Sellers of the *Sentinel* that he heard God's voice on his patio in 1994, saying just two words: "Clean Westerns." In a letter to Hill, Rev. Petero Sabune, a chaplain at Sing Sing Correctional Facility in Ossining, New York, wrote that the project's work is "helping inmates realize there is hope after prison." Some of the books are explicitly Christian, but others are simply escapist fiction. Whether or not the books lead those behind bars to religious conversion and transformation, "it's great to see them have good material to build them up rather than tear them down," said D. Lee Spell, a counselor at the Polk County, Florida, jail.

Some ministries and religious publishing houses—this one in particular—have made a veritable cottage industry with books and study guides examining the religious dimensions of ostensibly nonreligious novels, movies, and television series. Their approaches to these popular culture phenomena range from the analytical to the frankly evangelical. And their subjects range from the likely, *Lord of the Rings* and *The Chronicles of Narnia,* to the unlikely, *The Sopranos, The Simpsons,* and *Buffy the Vampire Slayer.* Perhaps the greatest stretch came in 2006, when Campus Crusade for Christ's Josh McDowell released *The Da Vinci Code—A Quest for Truth* (Green Key Books), with a first printing of 100,000 copies. The short paperback put an upbeat spin on Dan Brown's bestseller, in anticipation of the movie version starring Tom Hanks. McDowell refused to condemn Brown's novel, which was seen as anti-Christian by many, drawing heated criticism from Catholics, including the Vatican, and Protestants. "Let's see where fact leaves off and imagination begins," he told me, explaining that he wrote it for perplexed young Christians whose faith might be shaken. "It's a marvelous opportunity to be positive. The main purpose of my book is to reinforce their belief and placate their skepticism. If you look carefully, truth will always stand. . . . I look at the book and the movie as a platform for evangelism. A little controversy can be a marvelous tool."

As the phenomenal success of *The Passion of the Christ* at the worldwide box office demonstrated—nearly one billion dollars worldwide, including record-breaking DVD sales—evangelicals will go to the multiplex if there is something they want to see that reinforces (or at least does not undermine) their values. "Just as in the wider culture, evangelicals as a group are becoming more sophisticated in their interaction with popular culture," Robert K. Johnston, professor of theology and culture at Fuller Theological Seminary, told the *New York Times* on December 26, 2005. "There's been a recognition within the evangelical community that movies have become a primary means, perhaps *the* primary means, of telling our culture's stories. For this reason, evangelicals have become much more open to good stories, artfully told, but they also want stories whose values they can affirm and understand." In recent years, companies like Grace Hill Media and Motive Entertainment Partnership have sprung up in Hollywood to market studio films to Christian audiences. However, genuinely Christian-friendly movies are rare; it has been a long time since *Chariots of Fire*. So, what are suburban evangelicals who like movies to do to keep from staying home on weekends for lack of acceptable fare? Two coping mechanisms have evolved, each enabling Christians to more safely access commercial films, the movies their teenage children and their friends are talking about, like *Titanic* or *Spider-Man* (in which the Lord's Prayer is recited). The first is the rise of Christian and morality-based Web sites that rate, evaluate, and analyze new movies just as they go into commercial release. They have names like screenit.com, movieguide.org, hollywoodjesus.com, and christiancritic.com. Focus on the Family has pluggedinonline.com, Southern Baptists have moviereporter.com, and *Christianity Today* has christianitytoday movie.com. Each site, designed and maintained at relatively low cost, takes a slightly different approach. Some are clinical, listing every instance of objectionable language, nudity, sexuality, and violence. Others take a more thematic approach, weighing the value of the overall message against objectionable elements. In this way, moviegoers and parents can know what to expect when they go to the theater or drop off their children.

When they cannot find a credible alternative feature at their multiplex or accept what else is on the bill, some Christians initially adopted Procrustes' approach—cutting movies to fit their tastes, like the monstrous host in Homer's *Odyssey*. Companies, clustered in the states of Utah and Colorado, would purchase VHS and DVD copies of popular films, edit their content, and rent the expurgated versions to consumers. These companies had names like "CleanFlicks" and came into conflict with Hollywood studios. Directors and film industry organizations claim such companies distort and disfigure their work (although these "sanitized" versions are virtually identical to edits made subsequently for broadcast on network television or on airplanes), and the litigation over the issue commenced. Most recently, other companies like ClearPlay have introduced DVD players that work their alchemy on unedited discs, using embedded software that will automatically edit from view objectionable material from movies rented at chain outlets. "I like being able to watch movies in my own home without having that wince factor when something comes up," ClearPlay's president Bill Aho told Lucky Severson of public television's *Religion & Ethics Newsweekly* in September of 2005. "Nobody's comfortable seeing that little shot of nudity in the movies, not the kids, not Mom, not Dad." Stores like Wal-Mart specialized in selling such expurgated versions and technology, and they report especially strong sales in the South. In 2005 President Bush signed into law the Family Entertainment and Copyright Act. The law protects technology companies like ClearPlay's user technology from litigation based on copyright infringement (effectively ending the movie industry's pending litigation), but excludes from protection companies like CleanFlicks that are producing and marketing unauthorized, edited versions of commercial films.

What makes all this necessary? Why is there no Christian movie industry to rival the phenomenal success of Christian publishing? Evangelicals are trying to train their own writers, directors, and producers in programs with names like Act One, Reel Spirituality, and Art

Within Labs. The problem is cost. Books can be printed as they are sold, with little front-end risk. Film production is a high roller's game, risky in the extreme, with virtually no margin for error. It takes extraordinarily deep pockets and determination to make a successful film like *The Passion*. Taking a lower-key approach, Christian billionaire Phillip Anschutz is trying to do the same thing with his Walden Media production company, first with *Holes* and now with C. S. Lewis's *The Chronicles of Narnia: The Lion, the Witch and the Wardrobe,* a $150 million coproduction with Walt Disney Studios. The film has grossed more than $290 million, suggesting that *The Passion* was not a fluke. Frankly, consumers' standards are prohibitively high. With a presold market, the Left Behind series of novels was the first candidate to attempt to win over a mass-market audience for a Christian film. But the initial entry, *Left Behind*, featuring a cast of former television and minor film actors, lasted only a week in theaters, grossing an anemic $4.2 million, before going straight to video and DVD release—where it sold more than three million units. Notwithstanding, that experience did not prevent production of three more films based on the series, shot in Canada, and later released on video. Spurred by success of *The Passion,* and stung by Christian critics' ridicule of its previous efforts, the Left Behind production company bumped the budget for its October 2005 DVD release *Left Behind: World at War,* launching it with showings in thousands of churches the weekend of October 21–23, 2005. Another film based on the biblical Apocalypse, *The Omega Code,* with an $8 million budget, also had a brief run in theaters, grossing $12 million at the box office and producing a bigger budget sequel, *Megiddo: Omega Code 2,* which was a commercial failure. Both Omega films were made by Matt Crouch's Gener8Xion Entertainment, which announced plans in 2004 to make a feature based on *Hadassah: One Night with the King,* evangelist Tom Tenney's popular novel.

For many years, the Billy Graham Evangelistic Association, recognizing the emotional power of the big screen, produced its own films. But in most cases, these movies were not of sufficient quality to be released commercially. Instead, it was necessary to go from city to city, "four walling" the movies—renting out theaters for limited runs or showing them in churches. This approach survives today, and not just for Christians. In the autumn of 2004, backers of a full-length animated film called *Muhammad: The Last Prophet* rented theaters in thirty-seven U.S. and Canadian theaters. The limited run, the distributors acknowledged, was essentially a commercial for the subsequent DVD release of the children's movie, which told the story of Islam's founder.

But this way of exhibiting religious films has begun to change in the past decade, especially in 2004. *The Gospel of John,* produced by Canadian Garth Drabinsky, who is Jewish, and *Luther,* starring Joseph Fiennes and backed by several Lutheran denominations, were released commercially in 2003 and garnered respectful reviews. Compared to Gibson's *The Passion,* the results were modest. *The Gospel of John* and *Luther,* despite attempts to mobilize support among churches and on the Internet, did no better than break even at the box office. They may have greater long-term success, financial as well as evangelical, in video and DVD release and foreign exhibition. Similarly, an R-rated feature film based on a novel by African American evangelist T. D. Jakes, *Woman, Thou Art Loosed,* released in October of 2004, did not come close to *The Passion*'s success. Still, Jakes's contemporary movie, set in the inner city, earned about $7 million at the box office, easily earning back its $2 million production cost, thanks in part to the evangelist's appearance on *Oprah* and his own show on Trinity Broadcasting Network. *End of the Spear,* a $10 million film based on the true story of five young missionaries killed in Ecuador's Amazon jungle in 1956, and financed by Mart Green, a Christian businessman, earned back its investment at the U.S. box office in 2006—despite the revelation that the movie's co-star, Chad Allen, is gay and an outspoken activist—but quickly moved to DVD release.

The impact of film is especially dramatic when it comes to providing moral—if not specifically religious—instruction for young children. As I discussed in *The Gospel According to Disney: Faith, Trust, and Pixie Dust* (Westminster John Knox, 2004), Disney's animated features have filled this role in a general way for decades. Now, with the advent of cheaper, more sophisticated computer-generated animation companies like Pixar (now owned by Disney) and other studios like DreamWorks are churning out more family-friendly fare. But before *The Passion of the Christ,* the most striking breakthrough for Christians had been in the area of animated children's film. The phenomenon began in the early 1990s with a series of videos featuring primitive, cheeky computer-generated vegetables. Two Bible college friends, Phil Vischer and Mike Nawrocki, both puppeteers, called their Christian-oriented creations VeggieTales. Over the years an estimated five million families purchased more than thirty million units. The morality-based stories, featuring wisecracking characters like Bob the Tomato and Larry the Cucumber, built their following in Christian stores and church basements, outside traditional retail and media channels. In recent years, the growing, word-of-mouth popularity of VeggieTales has taken their videos, CDs, and merchandise beyond religious outlets—to major U.S. mass marketing and discount stores such as Target, Wal-Mart, Kmart, and Costco. The vegetables, Edward Gilbreath wrote in 2002 in the magazine *Christianity Today,* "have become celebrated symbols of evangelical ingenuity in popular entertainment, a realm in which Christians have struggled to be taken seriously." Until VeggieTales, he wrote, "there had never ever, ever been Christian-produced entertainment so funny and smart that viewers did not realize they were receiving moral instruction." This level of success culminated in 2003 in the release of *Jonah—A VeggieTales Movie,* a full-length animated feature, in nearly one thousand U.S. theaters. Taking a cue from Disney and DreamWorks, Jonah's release included a coordinated marketing campaign, with a complete array of merchandise—including a computer game and a fast-food tie-in with Chick-fil-A, a Christian-oriented, fast-food chain—connected to the movie. Equally significant is that reviewers for secular publications took the $12 million film seriously. Another *Christianity Today* writer, Douglas LeBlanc, made plain what was at stake with *Jonah*'s release. For years, he wrote, many evangelicals have dreamed of "a magic bullet: the one film that will make Hollywood moguls pay attention to us." *Jonah*'s ticket sales exceeded $25 million, which, alas, did not stave off bankruptcy and a subsequent takeover for its parent company.

Apart from commercial television shows like *Highway to Heaven, Touched by an Angel, 7th Heaven,* and, for two seasons, *Joan of Arcadia,* there have not been many successful network shows built around a religious or spiritual premise. Despite the failure of ABC-TV's *Nothing Sacred,* a drama about a troubled Catholic priest in the 1997–98 season, NBC-TV launched *The Book of Daniel* as a midseason replacement in 2006. That show, a more comedic take on a troubled

Episcopal priest who talks to Jesus, was also short-lived. (The denomination's official news service hailed the show for offering "the Episcopal Church a rare product placement opportunity.") High-quality alternative Christian television entertainment programming is scarce for much the same reason as the relative dearth of commercial feature films on such themes: front-end production costs. To many general television viewers, the term "Christian broadcasting" conjures up images of televangelists with poufy hair and weepy, overly made-up wives, begging for money. The audience rating shares for such shows, a majority of which air on independent UHF outlets or cable systems like Trinity Broadcasting Network, are comparatively minuscule. Although the production costs of television are no less daunting than the cinema, there have been a few efforts at creating "Christian alternatives" for commercial TV. Trinity, for example, began airing a "reality" show in 2003 called *Travel the Road,* based on the commercial series *Amazing Race,* which focused on the adventures of two twentysomething missionaries who traveled to twenty-five countries. In June of 2004 Trinity's Matt Crouch, son of the network's founders and producer of *Travel the Road,* launched a Christian version of Fox Television's *American Idol,* and there have been other knockoffs featuring gospel and contemporary Christian artists. Teamed with Orlando-based Johnny Wright, who managed the careers of sexy teen star Britney Spears and boy band 'N Sync, Crouch called his show *Gifted,* and aired on more than fifty independent commercial and religious stations, as well as on Trinity. One religious television network is producing its own (nonsteamy) soap operas. The PAX television network, which promoted family values in its early incarnation, owned sixty-five stations across the United States and was carried on many cable and satellite systems. Before entering into a problematic partnership with NBC, Jeff Sagansky, PAX's president and chief executive officer, said the network's goal, like that of founder Bud Paxson, is to be "uplifting" and "inspiring," although not explicitly religious. For example, the network had a long-running show called *It's a Miracle,* hosted by Richard Thomas, based on people's accounts of real-life, supernatural experiences. Other PAX series included *Doc* and *Sue Thomas: F.B. Eye.* Cloud Ten Pictures, which produced the two *Left Behind* films, announced plans to produce a television series in Canada based on the story and characters. In October of 2005, a church-centered sitcom called *Pastor Greg*, produced by Cornerstone Television, began airing on network affiliates and independent stations, as well as on religious systems like Cornerstone, Sky Angel, and Trinity Broadcasting Network.

The debate about appropriating popular culture for evangelical purposes has been going on for a long time, as I suggested above. I offer another example that is probably familiar—although possibly apocryphal. During the Protestant Reformation five hundred years ago, Martin Luther was attacked for cribbing tavern ballad melodies for his hymns. He is said to have retorted: "Why should the devil have all the good tunes?" This dialogue has continued—especially in the twentieth and twenty-first centuries—from jazz to rock to pop to hip-hop to rap. Is the beat of these various idioms intrinsically and irredeemably evil? Or can it be adapted and transformed? As Rick Warren puts it, "There is no Christian music; there are only Christian lyrics." Artists like Duke Ellington argued eloquently that jazz could become a mass. Perhaps the strongest current evidence that it can is the phenomenon known as Contemporary Christian Music, CCM for short. The genre—rock and pop music with Christian lyrics—has blossomed into a billion-dollar-a-year industry in the United States.

Here again, a key to CCM's success is the relatively low cost and incremental nature of production, which mirrors that of the publishing industry. CDs can be produced cheaply and in small numbers, and then turned out in larger numbers to meet whatever demand there is. Another factor has been the emergence of channels for promoting and distributing the product to its target market. Since the early 1980s, Trinity Broadcasting Network has aired the weekly show *Real Videos,* hosted by Matt Crouch, which showcases CCM videos. Numerous FM radio stations across the nation, both public and commercial, have adopted the CCM format. These are essentially rock stations, the only difference from secular stations being the lyrics and the beliefs of the people who work there. Thus, a Christian alternative allows children of the faithful to partake of the larger culture and not feel left out. In Orlando, for example, a Christian rock station, Z88.3-FM, which bills itself as a "positive alternative," and "Safe for Little Ears," is one of the highest-rated outlets of its kind in the nation, reaching an estimated 250,000 listeners a week and regularly finishing in the top ten in local ratings. And, as in the case of VeggieTales, Christian retail stores provide a ready outlet to market the music. Unlike secular chains and big-box stores, these outlets put a priority on CCM, because it is a major moneymaker. CCM's commercial success has made it a juicy target for lampooning. On Comedy Central's animated *South Park,* a show where scatology meets eschatology, one of the foulmouthed little characters cynically decides to form a Christian rock group, called Sanctified, just to cash in on a trend: "All we have to do is sing songs about how much we love Jesus, and all the Christians will buy our crap." On an episode of Fox's more benign *King of the Hill* called "Reborn to be Wild," the title character Hank Hill offers a similarly disparaging verdict on the genre: "You're not making Christianity better. You're making rock 'n' roll worse."

Apparently, almost no genre of popular culture is irredeemable—or too far out in left field—for evangelism. Costumed VeggieTales characters are a main draw for "Faith Nights" at minor league baseball parks, mostly in the Sunbelt, that draw large church groups. Kids cluster around Larry, the seven-foot cucumber, and his buddy, Bob the Tomato. Also included in the evenings are religious testimonies from athletes, Christian music artists, and biblical bobble-head dolls as giveaways (a practice mocked in a recent *Simpsons* episode). "Baseball, faith and Americana, it's a perfect fit," C. J. Johnson, director of marketing for the Hagerstown, Maryland, Suns, told *USA Today.*

There appears to be no limit to the trend of appropriating and adapting popular culture in the service of religion. With the possible exception of pornography, no genre is considered so intrinsically antithetical to Christianity that it cannot be put to positive use. Christians are now attempting—with some success—to adapt what is arguably one of the most sexual and violent genres of popular culture: computer games. The Christian computer game industry seems to be shadowing the rise of CCM, and for the same reasons. "Socially conservative Christians may not want their children to play video games at all," Billy Pidgeon, an analyst for Go Play Research, told *PC* Magazine in July of 2005. "On the other hand, when kids are asking to play video games, Christian parents may find these games an acceptable way to promote their values, while keeping their children entertained." Ben Turner, president of One Way Book Shops in St. Louis, agreed. "There is an extremely strong need for Christian video games that have more positive role modeling and morality wrapped around it to teach our younger generation," he told the *St. Louis Post-Dispatch* on January 7, 2006. "But the quality has to be at a level that competes with the current gaming systems that are out there." According to the *Wall Street Journal*, the sale of such Christian fantasy games may have hit $200 million in 2002 alone (although that is still a small fraction of the national market). Companies like Digital Praise, Brethren Entertainment, and N'Lightning Software have developed such games as "Victory at Hebron" and "Walls of Jericho," which are compatible with XBOX, PlayStation2, and GameBoy Advance. These alternatives run the gamut from childlike scenarios like "Charlie Church Mouse," who acts out Bible stories while wearing a T-shirt with a cross on it, and "The Bible DVD Game" to "Saint of Virtue," in which players wear the armor of God in order defeat inner enemies. For those who prefer more exciting battles, there is "Eternal War: Shadows of Light," in which players obliterate demons in the mind of a suicidal teen. Other games, with names like "Spiritual Warfare," "Catechumen," "King of Kings," and "Ominous: A Paladin's Calling," draw on the attractions of high-tech fighting (all in a good cause), the early persecution of Christians, and the mysteries of medieval times and the Dark Ages, according to the *Journal*. At least one California-based evangelical organization, Al Menconi's Ministries, has taken a page from the Christian movie review Web sites, setting up a system that rates video games. However, the audience for Christian video games may not yet have reached critical mass. "It just doesn't seem like there is a demand or an interest from the Church with these video game makers that they would come out with something that would be educating for our kids," Patrick Krepps, a youth pastor at Life Christian Center in St. Louis County, told the *Post-Dispatch*. "It always seems like we're behind in everything that's created for the public."

As unlikely as it may seem, evangelicals have managed to make both stand-up comedy and even the theme-park experience their own. In a May 2003 cover story entitled "Laughing for the Lord," *Charisma* magazine described sold-out concerts by performers such as "Gospel Komedy Slamm" in African American churches in Los Angeles. That same year, Promise Keepers, the evangelical men's group, added a Christian comic named Brad Stine to its nationwide lineup. In a scene easily mistaken for a cable television performance, the edgy, angry comedian prowled the stage in front of a an exposed brick wall, his pent-up aggression barely contained. A veteran of the club circuit, Stine railed at what he called our indulgent culture, "pagan" government, and the inconsistencies of political correctness: piety with a punch line. The market for Christian comedy has grown so much that there is an eighty-member organization called the Christian Comedy Coalition, and some comedy clubs have begun scheduling regular nights of religious humor. "Divine humor just may be the next big wave to burst on the Christian scene and beyond," according to *Charisma*. This, despite the fact that for years, "the idea of 'Christian comedy' was literally a joke," Mark Anderson, part owner of Improv comedy clubs in Phoenix, Dallas, and Washington, D.C., told the Pentecostal magazine. Testing the limits? There is also a Christian Wrestling Federation.

But just as evangelicals have appropriated various genres of modern popular culture, likely and unlikely, they have also adapted the most venerable and archaic forms: passion plays. This tradition—minus much of the virulent anti-Semitism and incitement to violence that characterized the European originals, like those at Oberammergau—survives in a uniquely American way in various parts of the Sunbelt, in settings as varied as Robert Schuller's Crystal Cathedral in Garden Grove, California, to a hillside in Eureka Springs, Arkansas. For innovation, however, few can compare with the annual "Story of Jesus" Easter passion play in the small central Florida community of Wauchula. The drama takes place several nights a week each spring, before two thousand people in the wooden bleachers of the Hardee County Cattlemen's Arena. In the course of the evening, a cast of more than two hundred people—thirty with speaking parts—and nearly that many animals, dramatizes the Gospels, beginning with Jesus' birth. In some ways the Floridians resemble the peasants of first-century Galilee who made up the bulk of Jesus' first followers— simple folk who made their living tending herds and bringing in the sheaves. Like the people they portray, Hardee County cast members are rural, faithful people of modest means and education, many of whom make their living from the land, growing fruit and vegetables and raising cattle. The local cowboys playing mounted Roman soldiers are clearly as skilled with their mounts as their historical counterparts must have been. Many of the elements from the New Testament follow in the Wauchula pageant: Jesus' ministry and miracles; his trial and bloody crucifixion; visitation by one angel ten feet tall on stilts and five other angels suspended from the ceiling, rolling in on wire tracks the length of the arena. As Jesus ascends to heaven, fireworks erupt at his shoulders. But in this play's conclusion, taken from an interpretation of the book of Revelation, Jesus comes thundering back into the rodeo ring on a white unicorn, wearing a sparkling gold crown and red cape, waving a sword. Emerging in black light from a cloud bank created by a row of fog machines, dodging fireworks and pillars of chemical smoke, he wheels his snowy steed onto the rise at center stage and rears up—and the crowd goes wild.

Concern with popular culture is neither a sectarian nor a partisan issue. Nonevangelicals are troubled by it as well, a fact that should not be lost on Democrats. For example, on December 13, 2005, Christian Brothers Investment Services, Inc., which manages more than $110 billion in investments held by mostly mainline Protestant groups, recommended guidelines for major U.S. retailers to keep video games rated "M" for mature out of the hands of customers younger than seventeen. There is no reason Republicans should have a monopoly on running against a soulless popular culture run by mercenary corporations. "These corporate Goliaths invest huge amounts of time and money thinking up ways to appeal directly to children, right over their parents' heads," wrote Barbara Dafoe Whitehead in her article for the Democratic Leadership Council. In the summer of 2005, when Susan Estrich, Michael Dukakis's campaign manager and now a cable pundit, criticized Senator John McCain for his cameo appearance in the raunchy sex comedy *Wedding Crashers,* Southern Baptist columnist Russell D. Moore praised her, despite his distaste for Estrich's feminism.

While I write a good deal about evangelical alternatives to popular culture, as a Jew I have little personal use for it. I find much of it insipid. However, as a parent, a media consumer and—in my heart—a blue-stater, I fully understand the impulse that has created it. It is ironic, I think, that, while some of their views may differ, the daily lives people in blue-state suburbs live closely approximate what evangelicals like to call "traditional family values." Many share evangelicals' revulsion at most of popular culture on moral grounds. To this, I would add my personal (elitist?) complaint: pop culture's relentless stupidity. On the whole I'm with the evangelicals on this issue. I am an unreconstructed '60s lefty, without apology or qualification, but when it comes to most of popular culture, I agree with the Southern Baptists: it's "of the devil" or, as our people put it, "drek." Commercial television is, as one radio evangelist put it, "the devil's story box." Its demeaning portrayal of women and parents and its trivializing view of sexuality are simply unacceptable to me. I don't want my kids watching mindless sitcoms and then talking back to me like sassy child actors—if I can help it. Call me a crank (and some have, including both of my offspring), but in this media environment, parents foolish enough to permit children to have a computer or television in their rooms, behind closed doors, have forfeited their right to complain when the inevitable transpires. When it comes to visual media, I have been a censor, but I am not a prude. There is no weeknight television viewing in our house during the school year, and there are no violent computer games—ever. At the same time, my children have watched *The Simpsons* on Sunday nights and during the summer since they were eight and eleven, and they now watch *South Park*. I have taken my son to quality R-rated movies since he was thirteen, and brought home for him a season's worth of HBO's *Deadwood*—because it presents serious issues and historical re-creations in intelligent and entertaining ways. During the summer, we are regular fans of *The Daily Show*.

As a First Amendment supporter—really—I have set a different standard for books and music. I have never banned a book or magazine or any reading matter, including graphic novels. Music is a closer call. I have voiced my concern about CDs with parental advisories, particularly with regard to misogyny, but I have never prohibited or returned a purchase. Once I did threaten—without following through—to require my son to read aloud the lyrics of a questionable rap CD at the dinner table.

And I did drag my son Asher along with me to visit one of the strangest places in Orlando, a Christian theme park.

Chapter 9

The Holy Land Experience

The Word Made Flesh

*O*rlando is a place where men and women dream big dreams, including grandiose visions about religion and faith. Some of these materialize: glass-walled megachurches, a Catholic shrine, worldwide ministries. But many more don't, like a live, year-round, $9 million musical production of *Ben-Hur* at the Orange County Convention Center that flopped. Others seem to succeed at first, only to crash and burn. A few dreamers are cast out of their own creations by the donors and supporters who helped build them. Marvin Rosenthal, born Jewish in Philadelphia and converted to Christianity, had two big dreams. For most of his adult life, he has worked to lead other Jews in the United States and Israel to Jesus, while at the same time educating Christians about the Jewish roots of their faith. And in late middle age, in order to help accomplish his first dream, he moved his ministry to central Florida to build a Bible-based theme park, the Holy Land Experience. If there is an expert on Marvin Rosenthal and the Holy Land Experience, I suppose I am it. At this writing, I have visited Holy Land more than two dozen times, producing nearly twenty articles for the *Sentinel* and pieces for two magazines, *Christianity Today* and *Moment,* a Jewish monthly. I've been interviewed on the subject by countless radio and television outlets around the country and around the world over the past seven years. This is the saga that embodies the divide between Jews and evangelical Christians, and how it is sometimes unbridgeable.

Rosenthal converted to Christianity as a teenager in the late 1940s, together with his brothers and mother, after their husband and father left their home and missionaries prayed with them. Marvin led a colorful early life, including a stint in the U.S. Marines and some time as a professional dancer. Ultimately, he married a Christian, was ordained a Baptist minister, and spent much of his early career as a pulpit minister and church speaker, ultimately joining the Friends of Israel Missionary and Relief Society in New Jersey, an old-line organization devoted to converting the Jews. These groups, like the Hebrew Christians, some with roots in the nineteenth century, were largely eclipsed by higher-profile efforts in the 1970s and 1980s, like Jews for Jesus and Messianic Jews, both of which tried to integrate Jewish ritual practice and Hebrew prayer with Christian theology—and all of which Rosenthal steadfastly opposed. After a doctrinal dispute with Friends of Israel, over the timing of the world-ending rapture, Rosenthal left to found his own ministry to the Jews, Zion's Hope, and moved to Orlando in 1989.

An engaging man with a pencil-thin mustache reminiscent of Clark Gable, a widow's peak, and an innate gift for showmanship, Rosenthal brought with him plans to build the ultimate religious roadside attraction along Interstate 4, not far from Universal Studios Florida. With small donations from individual Christians, together with large gifts from a few wealthy donors, he first built a headquarters for Zion's Hope—beige stucco in the Spanish mission style, dominated by a bell tower that quickly became a minor landmark. From that complex, he planned his dream for the Holy Land Experience, a "living museum" of first-century Jerusalem. When I first interviewed Rosenthal in his office in 1996, I had my doubts, which I have learned to keep to myself. Still, local Jewish leaders were upset enough to learn that a new national ministry devoted to converting the Jews to Christianity had sunk roots in central Florida. The idea of a theme park devoted to that goal was beyond their comprehension. Yet within five years Rosenthal's dream was a reality.

When guests enter Holy Land, Rosenthal promised, "They will leave the twenty-first century behind and embark on a journey that is unequalled anywhere in the world. It will be an experience that is educational, historical, theatrical, inspirational, and evangelical." Rosenthal turned to a professional theme-park design firm, ITEC Entertainment Corp., which has worked for the major attractions and for the Kennedy Space Center.

For a Saturday morning, the small, sunny market square in the Old

City of "Jerusalem" is quiet—almost too quiet. Nearby, the Temple Mount area is equally deserted: no Arabs, no Jews, no Israeli soldiers. The only noise before 10 a.m. comes from above, cars and trucks hurtling down I-4 toward Orlando's world-famous tourist corridor linking Disney World, Universal Studios, and Sea World. But even here, in central Florida's newest theme park, thousands of miles from the embattled region it tries to re-create, the Sabbath peace is short-lived. Soon tourists and curiosity seekers swarm through a massive entryway, modeled after Jerusalem's Lion's and Damascus gates, as they had in large numbers since the park's February 5, 2001, opening. They pay about thirty dollars apiece to feed tickets into high-tech electronic turnstiles like those at the other theme parks. Guides dressed as first-century residents of the Old City greet them with a hearty "Shalom." The scenes elsewhere in the park look innocent enough. A bearded man blows a shofar—the ram's horn—in front of a six-story representation of Herod's temple.

At the Holy Land Experience, the already pervasive Christian culture of America's traditional Bible Belt and the more aggressively evangelical forces of the modern Sunbelt collide—with a force that makes not just Jews, but even some Christians uneasy. The week the $16 million fifteen-acre attraction opened, there was barely controlled chaos. Paying customers had to be turned away as the park filled each day before noon. Under a winter sun, journalists and camera crews from around the world swirled through the crowds, searching for yahoos—anything that would make Americans look like morons, and cement Orlando's image as the capital of kitsch—with considerable success. Even the Israeli daily *Ma'ariv* and Israeli television showed up. Central Florida's talk radio was dominated by the opening.

Outside the park's front gate, the Jewish Defense League's Irv Rubin shouted insults about "soul-snatchers" through a bullhorn—a reference to charges that the park's primary goal was to lure unsuspecting Jews in hopes of converting them—making all the network newscasts. And, not surprisingly, jokes about Holy Land soon began to pop up on late-night TV, mocking the latest offering from the state that in 2000 couldn't run a proper presidential election. An episode of TV's *The Simpsons* caricatured an almost identical Bible-based theme park called "Praise Land," built by Homer Simpson's sometimes goofy evangelical neighbor, Ned Flanders. Why the furor? How was this theme park different from all other theme parks? The bizarre combination of religion and entertainment spectacle—the sacred and the trivial—accounted for much of the hubbub. The weather was nice, there were dramatic visuals, and no big national or international stories were competing for the headlines.

Even Rosenthal marveled that his "dinky" park was being compared to Disney's new California Adventure, which cost hundreds of millions of dollars and opened the same week at Disneyland in Anaheim. "I felt like I was holding onto a cyclone," he said later. "From my perspective, this is something God orchestrated," and Rosenthal made a persuasive case. Before actual construction on the park began, the city of Orlando decided to put a new interstate exit right across the corner of the property. The sale of the small parcel enabled Zion's Hope to recoup the cost of the entire fifteen acres. To add to this good fortune, several weeks before the opening, all the major commercial theme parks announced they were bumping their one-day adult admission cost to more than fifty dollars, making Holy Land's initial gate charge of seventeen dollars seem like even more of a bargain. But it was the more serious issue, involving central Florida's modest Jewish community of 30,000, that distinguished it from what would otherwise have been just another vest-pocket, second-tier tourist attraction, sans thrill rides, in an already crowded and competitive market.

The fuse was lit for the media storm in a preopening interview with Rosenthal I did for the *Sentinel*. He told me that any profits from the park would go to Zion's Hope and its missionary activities. My early reporting had raised questions about the appropriation of Jewish symbols, texts, and prayers at the park, beginning with its gift store, just inside the gate. The Old Scroll Shop was filled with skullcaps, prayer shawls, shofars, mezuzahs, menorahs, braided Havdalah candles, and Passover plates—all imported from Israel—along with official Israeli guidebooks to historic sites. The décor included a display of what appeared to be a lacquered section of Hebrew Scripture parchment. Among the books on display were some serious titles, like the Penguin Classics edition of Josephus's *The Jewish War,* Paul Johnson's *A History of the Jews,* and Thomas Cahill's *The Gifts of the Jews,* alongside such missionary titles as *Christ in the Passover.* I spotted *The Diary of Anne Frank* next to a biography of the apostle Paul, and

Chaim Potok's popular novel *The Chosen* opposite such evangelical materials as *What Every Jewish Person Should Ask,* promoting conversion to Christianity. Not so much an eclectic religious display, it seemed to be one lacing evangelical hooks with Jewish bait. Also crowding the shelves were music CDs in Hebrew and books produced by Messianic leaders like Mitch Glaser, of Chosen People Ministries. The hottest-selling piece of jewelry in Methuselah's Mosaics gallery was a silver star of David with a cross in the center. At the nearby Oasis Café, the menu on the wall—which included Goliath burgers and Hebrew National hot dogs—was posted on what looked like a stylized open Torah scroll.

Dramatic presentations at the park touched a deeper nerve with area rabbis. One, "The Wilderness Tabernacle," was a sophisticated sound and light show that mixed laser and special-effect fireworks to create a fiery pillar of light, along with taped narration, slides, and live actors in a faithful re-creation of the desert worship experience of the children of Israel following the exodus from Egyptian bondage. Much was taken directly from the book of Exodus, with such prayers as the Yom Kippur candle blessing, chanted correctly and, though no acknowledgment was provided, hinting at the participation of someone knowledgeable about Judaism. (At least one cantorial soloist, Beth Schafer of what is now the Congregation of Reform Judaism in Orlando, rejected a request to consult on the park's music.) But at the very end of the presentation came the hook: The narrator, speaking as an aged Levite priest, wondered if this sacred worship experience had merely been a "rehearsal," or a "shadow" of what was to come for the Jewish people. Then a slide of the nativity was spotlighted and a singer intoned, "Behold the lamb of God, who taketh away the sins of the world." Then the lights came up.

No rabbis were among the 150 clergy and others who previewed the park prior to its official opening. Whether this was just an oversight, as park officials insisted, or something more calculated, was never clear. Rosenthal says the invitations were not sent, but printed in his ministry's magazine, *Zion's Fire* (to which few if any rabbis subscribed). After the opening, the rabbis balked at paying their way in with money that would be used to evangelize Jews. Rabbi Daniel Wolpe, of the Southwest Orlando Jewish Congregation and at the time president of the Greater Orlando Board of Rabbis, was appalled when I described the use of Hebrew prayers. "That's disgusting," he said. "It's quite a different thing to create a monument that celebrates your tradition than it is to create a monument that is to be used to proselytize people outside of your tradition." But he and other rabbis, not having visited the park themselves, were in a bind when journalists began calling.

A joint statement was hammered out by the Jewish Federation of Greater Orlando in advance of the opening:

> The Orlando Jewish Community cannot condone what it understands to be the methods used by Zion's Hope and employed through The Holy Land Experience to achieve the Zion's Hope mission. . . . We call upon Zion's Hope to clearly announce to any visitor that funds collected from The Holy Land Experience may, ultimately, be used to proselytize Jews. . . . An honest dialogue would require that Zion's Hope notify visitors of this position.

However, the federation also urged central Florida Jews not to participate in the opening-day protest led by Irv Rubin, who flew in from Los Angeles; thus, only one local man showed up to join him. Inside the gate, Marvin Rosenthal gave scores of interviews to journalists, criticizing rabbis for prejudging what they had not seen. The minister claimed that Jews were themselves active proselytizers of their non-Jewish spouses, and compared the JDL to Nazis. When the questioning got tough, Rosenthal got even tougher, citing the low levels of synagogue affiliation of American Jews, estimating that 250,000 have abandoned their faith. He echoed sentiments made by members of a Jewish group, Jews for Judaism, that the only people who convert are those who do not find enough spiritual satisfaction and sustenance in the faith in which they were raised. People don't convert *from,* Rosenthal said, they convert *to.* As for the Jewish symbols and texts, he said, no one has a copyright on the Old Testament or on biblical Jewish history.

Standing at the periphery of these many interviews on opening day, I noticed something else that struck me as odd. Most of the media questions were not about proselytizing. And Rosenthal, a man who had devoted his entire adult life to bringing Jews to Jesus, was dodging and downplaying that goal. Rosenthal's purpose—to share the gospel with the Jews—was clear and unambiguous. He had repeated it in several interviews with me during the past four years—stressing it in his ministry's magazine and literature and, more critically, in fundraising materials aimed at the Christian evangelical community. The money raised to build the park came from a donor base cultivated for that purpose over more than a decade. One of the first guests through the turnstiles on opening day was Lloyd Locklier, a Bradenton, Florida, retiree and longtime financial supporter of Zion's Hope, who told me he saw the park's sponsoring ministry as "a mission to the Jews—to win them to Christ."

However, the image of a Christian theme park whose ultimate purpose is to draw Jews from their faith was not the one Rosenthal wanted to convey to the national and international media. So when reporters asked him if conversion of the Jews was his goal, he replied with studied sophistry. There would be no buttonholing or tract distribution on the grounds, he said firmly. "Visitors have every right to be left alone." The purpose of the Holy Land Experience was to be "a living Bible museum" and to share the good news of Christianity, "to sow the seed of the word of God," he said, adding that he was including—but not targeting—Jews. It was true, in a way. The park's promotional literature promises "a wholesome, family-oriented, educational and entertainment facility, where people can come and be encouraged, instructed and reinforced in their faith."

The reality was that Rosenthal needed Christian residents of central Florida and some fraction of the forty-three million tourists drawn to Orlando each year by the major theme parks to make his park financially viable. Yes, faith is often defined as the belief in things unseen. But in the Sunbelt, many evangelicals prefer something more concrete—and lifelike. A month after the park opened, Rosenthal insisted that Jews from around the world were visiting, despite the negative comments from Jewish and some mainline Christian leaders. Those who attacked Holy Land as a lure to gull unsuspecting Jewish visitors into converting missed the point: The park was designed to be a fundraising vehicle, almost entirely dependent upon Christian patronage, in order to bankroll Zion's Hope. That organization's sole, direct, and historic purpose was to "present Christian truth to the Jewish people and the Jewishness of the Bible to Christian people," in the words of its magazine, *Zion's Fire*. A Zion's Hope video sold in the gift shop put it this way: "As a missionary agency, Zion's Hope places personnel in strategic places throughout the world with the supreme task of reaching Jewish people in the world God so loves with the message of Christ's saving grace."

Indeed, after a while, Rosenthal's dissembling on this point became too much, even for some area Christian leaders, who complained that Rosenthal—under pressure, to be sure—was denying his life's purpose with the same vigor with which the apostle Peter denied Jesus on the eve of the crucifixion. A local Southern Baptist evangelist, who asked not to be quoted by name, said that Rosenthal's comments created a "credibility problem" in the Christian community. Within weeks of Holy Land's opening, its hiring practices also opened an additional rift among Christian groups. Word spread that Pentecostals and charismatics (who believe in ecstatic forms of worship like "speaking in tongues" and faith healing by "laying on of hands") need not apply for jobs at the park, not even to sell hot dogs. Pentecostal worship practices are anathema to fundamentalist Baptists like Rosenthal, though as many as half of evangelicals consider themselves Pentecostals or charismatic, especially in the South. "We are not charismatics," he said. "We love them. We appreciate them. But we would not offer them a job."

As might be expected, the whole idea of melding entertainment and evangelism also provoked criticism, some of it derisive, in the local press. When plans for Holy Land were first announced, one columnist suggested a ride called a Holy Roller Coaster. Another thought a better name for Holy Land might be Cross Country, or perhaps Six Flags over Israel, jibes Rosenthal shrugged off. "Our purpose was to spread the word of God," he told me a few years later, "but of course we needed to make it pay." More serious criticisms, some from other evangelical Christians, hit a nerve, especially from those concerned about Holy Land's potential to trivialize faith. Quentin Schultze, professor of communication at Calvin College and author of *Communicating for Life: Christian Stewardship in Community and Media* (Baker Books, 2000), said an attraction like Holy Land "makes religion more superficial and transitory" and contributes to a "consumerization" of faith. When people visit a tourist attraction, he said, they bring with them "a tourist mindset, which is: spend money and have a good time."

In the course of my first half-dozen visits to Holy Land, before and after the opening, I thought I had picked up every facet and nuance of the park and its message. But, at *Moment* magazine's suggestion, I made two more visits to the park with experts from different backgrounds: an Orthodox rabbi and a Catholic historian. The first thing spotted by Rabbi Sholom Dubov of the Chabad Congregation Ahavas Yisrael in Maitland was the Torah parchment mentioned earlier that was mounted on display in the gift shop. Park officials told me that it was a section from the scroll of Esther, purchased in the ancient Israeli city of Safed from a vendor. Actually, said Dubov, it was a section from Deuteronomy 13 and an ironic (or calculated) choice at that. The passage, he said, warned against any "false prophet" or "dreamer" who urges the worship of "other gods." The section later directs that anyone who urges the worship of idols should be stoned to death "because he has spoken in order to turn you away from the LORD your God." Rosenthal, who does not read Hebrew, said later that he knew what the parchment said but did not see the need to remove it because he did not consider Jesus to be a false prophet. Rabbi Dubov also noted how deceptive the music CDs were, mixing traditional Hebrew and Israeli songs and prayers with messianic messages. Might someone be taken in, I asked him? "It depends how knowledgeable a Jewish person is," he replied. The Wilderness Tabernacle spectacle, he said, was "basically accurate . . . but who is this geared to? There's no question in my mind that it's geared to Jewish people." If one assumes that, sooner or later, Jewish people will be exposed to the Holy Land Experience, the only problem would be Jewish ignorance of their faith, Dubov said. "It's no problem for a Jewish person with a healthy Jewish background." The use of other Jewish symbols was more troubling, Dubov said. "It does make us feel very uncomfortable when the shofar is used," a reference to the ram's horn sounded on Jewish holidays. The pitch for conversion is "shrouded," he said. Yet after a visitor spends two or three hours at Holy Land, "you're going to know that Christianity is the [intended] answer. . . . Let's call it what it is: bait for the Jewish people. . . . The clear thrust of Yiddishkeit is evident throughout the park."

John Dominic Crossan, a historian of first-century Christianity and cofounder of the controversial Jesus Seminar, moved to the small central Florida town of Clermont after his retirement from the faculty of DePaul University in Chicago. The author of more than twenty books, including *Jesus—A Revolutionary Biography* and *Who Killed Jesus?*

Crossan voiced concern about the park when I interviewed him by phone before the opening. Any depiction of Jesus' life and death that uses the New Testament as its sole source, rather than presenting a fuller context of available sources, ran the risk of appearing anti-Semitic, he said. The evangelical view of Jesus' crucifixion, he said, "is that the bad Jews convinced the good Romans to do their dirty work for them."

Several weeks later, as he toured the park, Crossan's fears were more than justified. He was impressed by some of the park's physical attractions and exhibits, including the façade of Herod's temple, which he call "a pretty good reproduction," and he termed the forty-five-by-twenty-five-foot scale model of ancient Jerusalem "first class." But a talk given at the model by a guide was more amusing than scholarly, he said, closer to a sermon than a lecture. Crossan, an Irish-born, former Catholic priest, called Holy Land "a commercial, not only for Christianity over Judaism, but for Protestantism over Catholicism." And as his visit wore on, Crossan became increasingly distressed by the content of the presentations. The Wilderness Tabernacle would have been more honest, he said, if it stated that the Levitical sacrificial traditions observed in the desert gave rise to two legitimate traditions in the years following destruction of the Second Temple—rabbinic Judaism and Christianity—rather than implying that one was superior to the other. Most disturbing were images in a movie, *The Seed of Promise,* shot in Israel in high-definition video. Images of a crucifixion are intercut with scenes of the Romans sacking the temple in AD 70. "It's a most ghastly justification for the destruction of Jerusalem," he said. The movie also depicts Roman soldiers appearing to spare from Jewish sacrifice a lamb—obviously Jesus. "A lamb saved by the Romans from being slaughtered? What's the message? The destruction of Jerusalem was God's vengeance, justice or retribution for the Jews' crucifixion of Jesus, the lamb. What the hell kind of God is that?" That interpretation came straight from the book of Matthew, Crossan said. "The Jews killed God, so the destruction of the Temple is God's judgment against them." Rosenthal reacted sharply when I conveyed this interpretation to him. "That was not in our mind," he insisted. "That was not what we're presenting in our film. . . . The Romans were responsible for Jesus' death."

For the Jews of Greater Orlando, the opening of the park was like poking a sharp stick at an old, unhealed wound. Why? Because, for many evangelicals in the South, winning a Jewish convert to Christianity is the brass ring, closing the circle after two thousand years of rejection—evidence that Jesus was the messiah. And some, including the Messianics, seemed to think the end justified the means—reaching out to Jews by blurring the distinctions between Christianity and Judaism, or with camouflage, by expressing love and political support for Israel. For Jews, this intermingling of Christian evangelism with support for Israel can be disorienting, and the evangelists know it. Zion's Hope's phone number is 1-800-4-ISRAEL. In a column (printed before the park opened) entitled "Secrecy and Deceit," in the *Heritage,* the weekly newspaper for the area Jewish community, retired Rabbi Rudolph J. Adler surveyed the religious landscape from the perspective of more than three decades in central Florida, particularly with regard to young people. "We have the Messianic Jews, Christian Athletes, Campus Crusades and other Conferences of Christian Men and Women who aggressively preach conversion of the Jews and to the Jews, and are making it very uncomfortable for Jews who are a small minority in America," he wrote. "The pressure on our young people is tremendous and comes to them at a time when they are still impressionable and not adequately schooled in their Jewish faith."

In recent years, central Florida's Jewish families have found copies of Campus Crusade for Christ's "Jesus Video" in their mailboxes, as part of a citywide campaign to reach every household in the Orlando area. In 1999, in the adjoining suburbs of Winter Park and Maitland, families with Jewish-sounding names received personal invitations from a small Baptist church to a "Support Israel" Sunday service. Those who did not respond received follow-up phone calls. The service was advertised as featuring "Jewish style music," "Jewish specialty items," and a sermon by Rev. Rylan Millett on "Why we should thank God for Israel and the Jewish people." (The response from area rabbis was to criticize the campaign in their own sermons.) "There is nothing more offensive to Jews than to be proselytized," Rabbi Wolpe told a March 2001 luncheon meeting on Holy Land and Jewish-Christian relations at College Park Baptist Church in Orlando. "We are very sensitive to being told to convert. It doesn't convert us. It annoys us."

"The Holy Land theme park touched off a visceral reaction against evangelicalism," wrote *Heritage* columnist Dan Coultoff. "Orlando's rabbis have offered clear, heartfelt explanations about why Judaism is irreconcilable with belief in Jesus as the Messiah. . . . But defeating evangelicalism over the long haul, and reversing the rise of unaffiliated and uninvolved Jews requires . . . something more." Jews also need to be aware of deceptive groups and practices, according to Mark Powers and Scott Hillman of Jews for Judaism's Baltimore office. The two men visited Holy Land the weekend after it opened, at the federation's invitation, and discussed their findings with large student and adult audiences at two Jewish congregations and a Hebrew high school. "Don't be fooled," Powers warned them. "Don't let someone trick you into not being Jewish." Eric Geboff, the federation's executive director at the time, acknowledged that "there was a lot of anger. . . . The questions were all over the place: 'How do we protect our teens on college campuses?' 'Why are they doing this to us?' 'Why don't they leave us alone?'" These people come in and appear to be so knowledgeable, Geboff added, and many Jews "don't know how to respond when they talk about messiah."

As a result, the Federation's Community Relations Council made responding to Christian evangelism in general, and Holy Land in particular, a priority in 2001. They worked with non-Jewish and ecumenical groups like the National Conference for Community and Justice to quietly discourage public schools from planning field trips to Holy Land. "What I'm hearing from rabbis is that most of their mainline Christian friends and colleagues are as angry about this as we are," Geboff said. "They see evangelism as threatening to their congregations also." Some Jews in central Florida hoped their children would respond the way sixteen-year-old Sarah Milov, a Jewish tenth-grader did. Milov, a member of Ohev Shalom, a Conservative synagogue, was then attending a Christian school, Trinity Preparatory School, which is affiliated with the Episcopal Church. So the article she wrote for *Rave,* a weekly teen supplement to the *Orlando Sentinel,* was telling: "The entire premise" on which the park is based— conversion of non-Christians—is "antithetical to Jewish teachings," she wrote. While clearly designed to convert Jews, she told me in an interview, the theme park had the opposite effect on her. "Instead of tempting me, it made me say, 'Boy, this isn't for me.'" She also found the attractions "incredibly lame." It was, Milow wrote, "a bastardization of any faith to turn it into a theme park." And, although alarm continued in the Jewish community, there were those who took a longer view of history, maintaining that Jews have little to fear from Holy Land. Mike Nebel, a son of Holocaust survivors and a longtime activist in the local Jewish community, took the fuss over Holy Land with a grain of salt. "We've survived the fall of civilizations, pogroms, and the Holocaust," he said. "We'll survive here."

In the years that followed, there were ups and downs in the relationship between Holy Land and the Jews. There were signs of deference to Jewish sensitivities, although they may be coincidental. An announced plan to add a live drama of Jesus driving the money changers from the temple, one of the more inflammatory and arguably anti-Semitic episodes in the New Testament, never materialized. And the annual Easter season reenactment of Jesus' crucifixion was constructed to begin with the Via Dolorosa, eliminating the equally controversial scenes of crowds of Jews calling on Pilate to execute Jesus.

But in 2002, Holy Land expanded, opening an additional attraction, a $9.5 million "Scriptorium" to hold part of the biblical antiquities collection of the late Chicago financier Robert D. Van Kampen, valued at $20–100 million. In addition to paying for the domed, copper-sided structure built to resemble a Byzantine basilica, the Van Kampen Foundation agreed to loan the Scriptorium its twelve thousand artifacts and manuscripts. These included Babylonian cuniforms from 2200 BC; a Coptic Bible from fourth-century Egypt; a 1611 King James Bible; and another from one of Gutenberg's presses. What troubled Jews in central Florida and further afield was the announcement that the Van Kampen collection also included ten to twenty complete Torah scrolls—containing the Five Books of Moses—and fragments of others, including one from the historic community of Kaifeng, China. I knew that over the centuries many Torahs had been stolen and looted, and that during World War II the Nazis had seized hundreds, if not thousands of sacred scrolls from European synagogues and communities. So naturally, in writing my story announcing the Scriptorium for the *Sentinel,* I asked the foundation's officials and curators for the provenance of the Jewish artifacts. To my amazement, they said there was none, raising serious questions about the manner in which they had been acquired. This raised a larger issue. "A Torah should not be a display item," said Rabbi Wolpe, regardless of how it is acquired. "It is a holy item, and it should be used in this way. If a synagogue took a holy item of another faith and displayed it like it was a museum piece, the other faith would be justifiably upset. We would be justifiably upset to see something holy to us used as a museum piece." Rosenthal's response was that he had seen plenty of Jewish ritual art on display in museums in Israel.

There were other controversies involving Holy Land, some not involving the Jews. Orange County tax assessor Bill Donegan ruled that the property was a tourist attraction and theme park, rather than a nonprofit educational and cultural facility. This forced Rosenthal to file suit, which was ultimately successful, the court ruling that Holy Land had been denied due process. Donegan vowed to appeal the decision, he said, in order to avoid setting a precedent for other religious organizations who might want to start their own attractions. But the biggest problem—one that wouldn't go away—was that the competition for the tourist dollar in Orlando is brutal and unrelenting. Holy Land's big crowds following the opening—308,000 in the first eleven months, according to Rosenthal—melted over time, especially during the unbearably hot and humid summer months. When the attraction opened, Rosenthal said it would need 180,000–200,000 visitors per year to break even. For four and a half years, except for a severe drop following the terrorist attacks of September 11, 2001, Rosenthal said that Holy Land averaged 220,000 visitors a year. The three hurricanes that struck central Florida in 2004, while doing relatively little physical damage to Holy Land, devastated ticket sales. To compound the cash flow problems, Marvin and his son David drove up operating costs by commissioning and rotating new live musical and dramatic presentations throughout the park; boosting the park's payroll to two hundred when attendance was high; and adding displays of animals, including camels. There was talk that Marvin was distracted by the religious services, seminars, and conferences he ran in Zion's Hope's auditorium and by the trips he led to Israel. According to Internal Revenue Service documents filed by Zion's Hope for 2003, the most recent year available for the nonprofit, the ministry had income of $8 million and expenses of $8.5 million, the difference made up by loans and donations. The parting of the ways came on July 20, 2005.

Despite such a promising start, things did not end well for Marvin Rosenthal and the Holy Land Experience. The dreamer was expelled, albeit with a separation agreement, was asked to clean out his desk, and left Holy Land as its chief operating officer. Also departing were his wife Marbeth, his son David, and his brother Stanley. "We just had a difference of opinion, the board and I," Marvin told the *Sentinel*'s Jerry Jackson. Holy Land was taken over by Scott Pierre, Van Kampen's son-in-law, head of the Van Kampen foundation, and also chair of the theme park's board. Pierre said the vote to dismiss the Rosenthals was unanimous. "Marv's strength really was in the ministerial arena," he told the *Sentinel*. The board intended to help Rosenthal start a new ministry, Pierre said. That might come in handy. Marvin's salary for 2003, according to the IRS documents, was only $51,000, plus a $27,000 housing allowance, ranking him about third in compensation among Holy Land's staff.

I think that what happened to Marvin Rosenthal is that his second dream, Holy Land, eclipsed his first dream, converting the Jews. In one *Sentinel* article I wrote, I compared Rosenthal to a circus ringmaster, suggesting the only thing the showman lacked was a top hat. He liked the image so much, I later heard, that he thought about going out and buying one. A month after he left Holy Land, we sat down for breakfast at a restaurant across the interstate from the park. He was—by turns—rueful, combative, defensive, and philosophical as we reviewed the previous nine years. "I believe I was an able administrator and a good CEO," he said, while refusing to criticize Pierre or the board. If he made a serious mistake, he said, it was treating the expanded park staff as his mission family, which made him reluctant to make cutbacks when attendance declined. He still wished local rabbis had come to Holy Land to see the Wilderness Experience. With great feeling, he told me he would have opened the park at night for them without charge to avoid controversy and wouldn't have minded if they left before the controversial final minutes of the Christian message. The park could still succeed, he said. If it expanded, and operators could figure out more activities for children, it could ultimately draw 600,000–800,000 visitors a year. Perhaps. But on October 13, 2005, Holy Land's new executive director, Day Hayden, announced that the park would be closed on Sundays, "to give the staff of 225 time to spend that day in worship with their families," according to that day's *Orlando Sentinel*. Not coincidentally, the action would also reduce operating expenses.

Conclusion

Stranger in a Strange Land

*O*ne of the pleasures of covering religion for a Sunbelt newspaper is that I have become a Johnny Appleseed of books. Because I write about faith, and sometimes about the publishing industry that has grown up around it, I am inundated with new volumes on subjects both incisive and arcane. Some are so obscure I wonder why trees died to create them—a thought I hope you are not entertaining about the work you are now holding. My friend Nancy Pate, the *Orlando Sentinel*'s longtime book editor, once explained to me that a university or denominational publisher could actually do pretty well financially with titles that sell only 3,000–4,000 copies. In other words, the industry's economics of scale and low or nonexistent author advances facilitate publishing proliferation. There is no way I can read—or store—more than a fraction of the books I receive. So what I do is to sort them by religion, theology, and denomination and pack them into plastic bins. Then I load them into the back of my battered (but paid for) Volvo station wagon. Whenever I pass a local seminary, ministry, house of worship, or administrative office, or have lunch with a member of the clergy, I invite friends and acquaintances to take their pick—with the proviso that I might later want to pick their brains about the books. Matching just the right books to the right readers is a joy.

The twelfth-century Jewish physician and philosopher Maimonides—Rabbi Moshe ben Maimon—wrote a classic text for his co-religionists called *A Guide for the Perplexed*. With respect for, and apologies to the Sephardic sage, I wrote this particular book, too, as a guide for the perplexed. That is, for Jews (and, to a lesser extent, mainline Christians) in blue states who are baffled by the recent—and apparently inexorable—rise to political influence of evangelicals, many living in Sunbelt states that voted Republican in 2000 and 2004. I acknowledge that some blue-staters and old comrades on the left, who expected a tougher, in-depth critique or a searing expose of evangelicals from me—given my personal politics and history—may be disappointed. But that would be a book for another time, and perhaps for another author (In the meantime, I recommend Rabbi James Rudin's *The Baptizing of America: The Religious Right's Plans for the Rest of Us* [Thunder's Mouth Press, 2006]). Rather, this is meant as an introduction for the uninitiated, painted with a broad—and somewhat forgiving—brush. Or perhaps an opportunity for evangelicals to see themselves as another sees them.

It is probably true that in some ways—culturally and politically, to be sure—I would be more comfortable living among the people I am writing for, in Cambridge or on Manhattan's Upper West Side, or in a southern college town like Durham or Chapel Hill. But it has not been unbearable here: we have home delivery of the *New York Times,* two public radio stations, the BBC, a college, two growing seminary branches, and a rapidly expanding state university. And my evangelical friends and neighbors are good people, with much to admire about them. For example, when a racist, skinhead newspaper was distributed on my street, Reed McCormick, an Episcopal priest who lives two doors up, walked from driveway to driveway picking them up so we wouldn't see them. Too, I am in awe of Southern Baptists— their courage, dedication, and professionalism in the face of natural disasters. They are the shock troops of disaster response, ready to march into hell armed only with Bibles, chainsaws, and mobile kitchens. Evangelicals are among the most loyal people on earth. Treat them fairly—which does not automatically mean favorably— and they will never forget it.

There are some things I don't like about some evangelicals: the double standard on the moral conduct of some of their leaders (Ralph Reed, former head of the Christian Coalition, and his involvement with corrupt lobbyist Jack Abramoff comes to mind), and the way too many automatically attribute the worst motives to liberals and Democrats. And why? After all, as no less an evangelical than Rick Warren points out, the mainline Christian liberals were way ahead of fundamentalists and evangelicals on the last century's great moral issues like civil rights for African Americans, ending apartheid in South Africa, and equal treatment for women; and progressive Christians have been faithful and steadfast allies on helping the poor. If I could change anything about many evangelicals, I would like to find some way to pull them out of a mindset that assumes that everyone is like them: white, English-speaking, and believers in their flavor of Christianity. And their assumption that power and authority should naturally be in male hands. So, too, I wish they would be a little more discerning in their political choices. I look forward to the day when a Sunbelt politician will have to do more to get elected than simply to climb on a Ten Commandments monument, wrapped in a Confederate battle flag, and scream "terrorism" and "gay marriage."

Some years ago, Steve Brown, a conservative evangelical whose radio commentaries from my home town of Maitland are heard on more than six hundred stations, was paired with liberal Tony Campolo on the Odyssey cable network show called *Hashing It Out.* The two agreed on very little in the area of politics and economics, as one might expect. But they enjoyed the exercise in evangelical diversity. It demonstrated, Brown told me, "how people can disagree and still love each other." Steve, who has become my friend, is right. Rick Warren calls this the "culture of civility." Conservative columnist Cal Thomas and liberal commentator Bob Beckel seem to manage it in their "Common Ground" feature in *USA Today.* Doug Muder, writing in the Unitarians' magazine *UU World,* echoed Steve Brown, but from the left. "We need, in short, to reclaim one of Christianity's best ideas and hardest practices: We need to love our enemies and bless with hope those who curse us with anger. Such love and such blessing would not be a sign of weakness or an overture to surrender, but rather a portent that we had found the true power of our religious heritage. Armed with that power, we can win these culture wars. Without it we may not deserve to."

So, are there some principles relating to life, work, faith, politics, and culture—some rules of civil engagement—that might help us through this otherwise divisive period of struggle? Back in the 1960s some of us in the New Left borrowed (or appropriated) a slogan from the Old Left of the 1930s: "There is joy in struggle." Admittedly, these words may simply be a rationale for fighting the good fight—and losing.

(Remember that line from '60s political satirist Tom Lehrer's album *That Was the Year That Was*, about the Spanish Civil War: "They won all the battles, but we had all the good songs"?) I think there still can be joy in moral struggles that give meaning to our lives. While asking people to love their adversaries may be asking a bit much, especially for us non-Christians, respect may be a more realistic goal. Consider these as a starting point:

- Seek to understand your intellectual and philosophical adversaries' views and why they hold them. Read what they write and try to learn what experiences have shaped their lives and outlook.
- Build friendships with these adversaries. Take someone from the other side to lunch. You may find that they have hopes or kids or job hassles or hobbies or mortgages or family illness or aging parents or disappointments or victories or memories or childhoods—or all or most of the above—much like your own. Sometimes discovering common connections can breed understanding and civility, even bonding.
- Ratchet down the rhetoric. If you're not a talk-show host, you don't have to sound like one. Before writing or speaking ill of your adversaries, ask yourself if you'd say the same things as a guest at their family dinner table. Or maybe go one further. Imagine that you were a dinner guest in the home of an intellectual or political adversary who had young children. Now think ahead forty years. How might those grown children recall you? With fondness and respect or disappointment and disdain?

I said in the introduction that with my move to central Florida my education had begun in the ways of evangelicals in the Sunbelt suburbs. "Where is it now?" my friend Ernie Bennett asked not long ago. I'm not sure. I think it is continuing. Frankly, I still cannot predict what in an evangelist's message or delivery makes it break through to national prominence or the bestseller list. Both my son Asher and my friend T. D. Allman have suggested that, in the process, I may have become a victim of the "Stockholm syndrome," that I have been in the thrall of evangelicals for so long that I have become their sympathetic hostage. Each points to the fact that I seem to be wearing my hair in a poufy way, like a TV preacher. Well, I like it that way—*somebody say amen!* Just kidding. But I do admit it is a complicated relationship that I am still trying to muddle through. Stay tuned.

A curious road took this Jew from Jersey all the way to the First Baptist Church—and lots of others—in Orlando and beyond. Along the path, I've found myself educated, enlightened, amused, entertained, dismayed, and sometimes even flummoxed. As a journalist, I've seen that in order to truly understand a political interest group or religious movement, it helps to go beyond interviewing the leaders or even conversing with the followers. Knowing grass-roots adherents personally as friends and neighbors can make a huge difference. My fellow journalists frequently look not only for an angle but also an edge, not just a salient social connection for their story but also an advantage in communicating it. Cultural immersion—the opposite of the cultural disconnect that has characterized the nation's culture wars—can facilitate both. The same would seem to apply in many professional arenas in which communication is essential: politics, education, business, government, medicine, the service professions, and more. And isn't it true of life in general, both in nations and neighborhoods? If the stories you've read here can help people communicate with understanding and civility—or even begin to think about doing so—maybe these tales can contribute to both public and personal good. I'd be honored and humbled, were it so.

Suggested Reading

Micklethwait, John, and Adrian Wooldridge. *The Right Nation: Conservative Power in America.* New York: Penguin Press, 2004.

Wacker, Grant. *Heaven Below: Early Pentecostals and American Culture.* Cambridge: Harvard University Press, 2003.

Webber, Robert E. *The Younger Evangelicals: Facing the Challenges of the New World.* Grand Rapids: Baker Books, 2002.

Wilson, Charles Reagan, and Mark Silk, eds. *Religion and Public Life in the South: In the Evangelical Mode.* Religion by Region Series. Walnut Creek, CA: AltaMira Press, 2005.

Wolfe, Alan. *One Nation, after All: What Middle Class Americans Really Think about God, Country, Family, Racism, Welfare, Immigration, Homosexuality, Work, the Right, the Left, and Each Other.* New York: Penguin Group, 1998.

Wolfe, Alan. *The Transformation of American Religion: How We Actually Live Our Faith.* Chicago: University of Chicago Press, 2003.

Acknowledgments

This book began as an essay in the January/February 2005 issue of the *Columbia Journalism Review,* a publication I have written for since the early 1970s. In the days following the 2004 presidential election, I thought I should speak to my colleagues in blue states, who seemed to be going through some serious times of recriminations about somehow "missing" the role of evangelicals, the election's "big story." Gloria Cooper, *CJR*'s deputy executive editor and longtime managing editor, immediately liked my approach, and the essay dropped right into the magazine's "Voices" section. When the issue appeared, my piece was widely linked on evangelical Web sites, and my editor at Westminster John Knox Press, David Dobson, suggested it might be expanded into a short book. So, to Gloria—a long-distance colleague for thirty years—and executive editor Mike Hoyt and David, thank you all.

In growing the essay to book length, I have tried to rely primarily on my own observations and reporting for the *Orlando Sentinel* and other publications. If I emptied my notebooks, I think there were some interesting things in them. However, in writing about events that I was unable to cover in person, I have also drawn extensively on the writing of my colleagues of the Religion Newswriters Association, in particular Laurie Goodstein of the *New York Times* and Paul Nussbaum of the *Philadelphia Inquirer.* Thus, if in places I have cut-and-pasted, the clips I used in doing the job were excellent, and I have given proper credit.

For the third time as an author, I first went for advice and counsel

154 Acknowledgments

to Rusty Wright, my friend from Duke undergraduate days and now an author and speaker. As he was the initial reader of my previous manuscripts, I knew his advice was critical, and it has been, helping to distill my thoughts while leavening them with his insights, especially in the first and last words. Peter Brown, my good friend and (now former) *Orlando Sentinel* colleague, provided a vigorous, tenacious neocon perspective that challenged me, and strongly suggested the need for a chapter profiling the three evangelical families. Other return readers include Rev. Ernest Bennett, canon to the ordinary of the Episcopal Diocese of Central Florida, and Mark Andrews, also of the *Sentinel,* who were likewise acute. Of all my regular readers, I think Clay Steinman, a friend and comrade of more than thirty-five years, gave me the hardest time and was the most disappointed. Still, I expected no less and I thank him. This time around, I had two new readers: Reggie Kidd, of Reformed Theological Seminary; and John Harbison, my beloved twelfth-grade U.S. history teacher at Pennsauken High School, and reconnected friend. Numerous others read individual chapters, and Lawrence Pinkham, another beloved old teacher, from the Columbia J-school, made a small but valuable contribution.

Others at the *Sentinel,* where much of the reporting for this book was done, have provided a consistently supportive work and social environment. They accommodated and tolerated (as best they are able) my book writing and subsequent and ferocious self-promotion. Chief among these are my writing colleagues in the news features department and throughout the paper, including lunch companions Hal Boedeker and Jay Boyar. My former editor, Loraine O'Connell, could always be depended upon to rescue my sometimes-muddled newspaper writing and was kind enough to read this manuscript. Editors up the line who have been extremely helpful, and often indulgent, include Barry Glenn, Kim Marcum, Bob Shaw, Mark Russell, and Charlotte Hall. On the corporate side, Ashley Allen and our good-hearted and straight-talking publisher Kathy Waltz also have my gratitude.

Duke University, my alma mater, was gracious enough to name me the inaugural Divinity School media fellow, which enabled me to draw on the resources of their faculty in the final stages of preparation of this manuscript. Kelly Hughes of DeChant-Hughes & Associates has done yeoman service in flogging my books and speaking engagements.

This is a short book, so I know I should keep the acknowledgments brief as well. I owe the greatest thanks to my family. I am not the easiest guy in the world to live with, believe me, so love and thanks to Sal, Liza, and Asher. Also to my brother, Paul—my personal candidate for president—and my in-laws, Charlotte Brown and the late Joe Brown, who was a wonderful and supportive presence in my life for twenty-five years.